DAD'S GUIDE TO RAISING TWINS

How to Thrive as a Father of Twins

Joe Rawlinson

dadsguidetotwins.com

Dad's Guide to Raising Twins: How to Thrive as a Father of Twins

ISBN-13: 978-1507584996
ISBN-10: 1507584997

Published by Texadero LLC, Austin, Texas

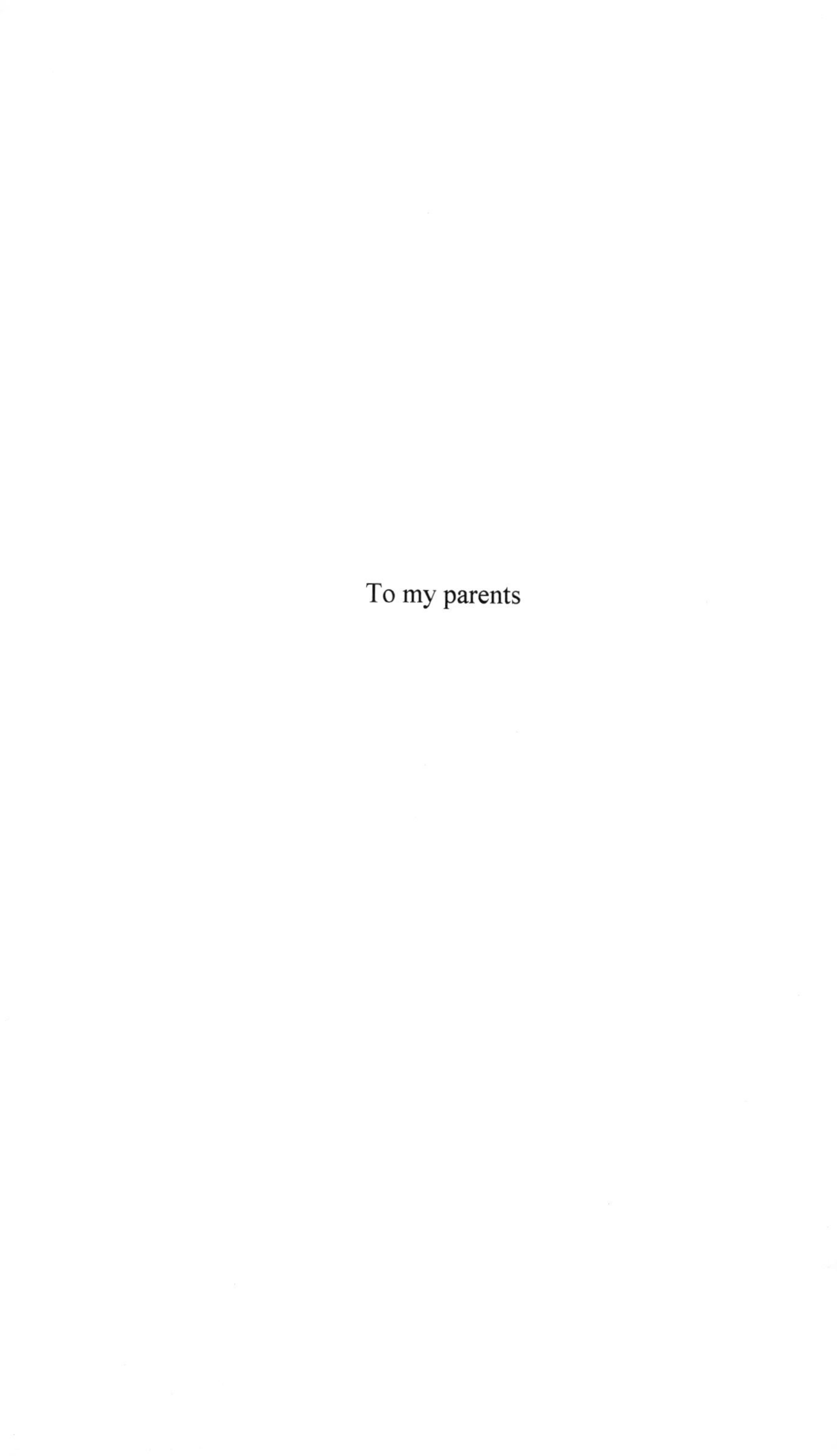

To my parents

WHY THIS BOOK?

There are countless books on parenting children, even some tailored for dads. However, raising twins is a unique endeavor that requires special discussion and treatment.

Even when you move to the specialty twin books for parents, dads are mostly relegated to the footnotes.

When my wife and I were expecting our twins, I couldn't find any great sources of information for dads expecting twins. I figure if I had that trouble, other fathers like you probably need information, too. I wrote my original "Dad's Guide to Twins" book so you could learn from my experiences, survive the twin pregnancy, and prepare for your twins' arrival.

Being ready for twins is one thing, actually raising them is another. Once you bring your newborn twins home, you have a whole new world to conquer.

I realized that while my first book goes into great depth on the twin pregnancy and preparing for your twins, you need more information on how to actually raise twins once you bring them home and start living each day as a father of twins.

This book covers all aspects of raising twins during those early years.

ABOUT THE AUTHOR

I'm Joe Rawlinson, the father of four children: two boys and identical twin girls. When our twins were born, our boys were three years old and 21 months old.

We proudly proclaimed that we had four kids ages three and under. That proclamation quickly gave way to the reality of caring for those four kids. Needless to say, we had our hands full and still do!

Having and raising twins is an awesome adventure. I just wish I knew what I know now before we brought our girls home and had to figure everything out as we went along. I've taken what I've learned and have helped thousands of parents of twins (like you) through my original "Dad's Guide to Twins" book, blog, podcast, and writing.

I'm pleased to share with you now some of my experiences (and those of others, too) as you move into the next phase of being a twin dad.

You'll find all the resources mentioned in this book and several free bonuses at www.dadsguidetotwins.com/more

DISCLAIMER AND FINE PRINT

The tips and insights offered in this book are based on my own experience and research. There may be inaccuracies, errors, and even a heavy dose of my own opinion.

I'm not a doctor. Be sure to consult with your twins' pediatrician and your wife's doctor on all health matters. I'm not an accountant or lawyer either, so on financial and legal matters, double check with them, too.

Every set of twins is different and your experience will be different from mine. In fact, I hope it will be better if you implement some of my tips and advice.

TABLE OF CONTENTS

CHAPTER ONE

The Journey Begins

It was supposed to be just another regularly scheduled doctor visit during my wife's twin pregnancy. She was 36 weeks pregnant with our twin daughters. By this stage of the pregnancy, my wife was "done". She was ready for the babies to be here. They just weren't ready to come out yet. Or so we thought.

During the visit, the doctor hooked up a contraction monitor to my wife. Even though my wife couldn't feel it, she was contracting. Her body was getting ready to expel our little babies into the world.

That simple doctor's visit turned into us heading directly to the hospital for labor and delivery.

Surprisingly, we weren't ready for that. We had assumed our doctor visit would just be a checkup with orders to return in another week. The hospital bag was back at home. I was sick with a cold.

While we were caught off guard, we weren't about to delay our twins' delivery. After several hours waiting for our doctor and the operating room, my wife was prepared for her C-section.

Our girls arrived two minutes apart. One was white as a ghost and slightly smaller than her flush, red in the face, bigger (yet younger) sister.

With their birth I was instantly a member of the father of twins club. I had eagerly awaited that moment with both fear and excitement since we found out we were having twins. Now they were here. What was I supposed to do?

We had prepared a lot for our twins' arrival and were confident in our preparations. However, the reality of caring for twins was more difficult than I could have imagined.

As Charles Dickens stated, "it was the best of times, it was the worst of times." Even though he wasn't talking about newborn twins, he very well could have been!

We were overjoyed to welcome our girls into the world. We were happy they were healthy.

Then we brought them home and reality struck.

The challenges of caring for twins and two toddler brothers were overwhelming. An endless cycle of feedings, sleeping, and diapers lay before us. We struggled through crying and feeding at all hours of the day. We tried to console inconsolable twins. We felt the brunt of learning to parent two at the same time.

I've heard from several fathers of twins who compare the first week with twins to the Hell Week that Navy SEALs go through as part of their training. Endless stress, sleep deprivation, and physical demands that break even the strongest of men. Yes, that sounds like twins.

Despite the craziness of twins, it is awesome being a father of twins if you focus on the positives.

How to Find Joy in the Journey with Twins

It's true that twins are exhausting and are a lot of work. During the first year with infant twins, it's crazy-busy, and it's a blur. In addition to the day-to-day care of twins, you freak out about the financial aspect of twins.

If you don't put all those things to the side and focus on the big picture with your twins, you're going to get depressed and overwhelmed. Fortunately for you, there are a lot of amazing things about being a dad of twins. I'll share some of the experiences that I have had with my twin girls so you can look for the bright side of having twins. Know that you have something to look forward to in this amazing journey. You can find joy in the journey with twins.

Witnessing the birth of my twin daughters was incredible and marvelous. I'd seen the birth of our singleton boys before, but of course they came one delivery at a time. The twin pregnancy was surreal leading up to the delivery. Yes, my wife was bigger than with our individual boys, but I sometimes doubted: "Wow. Are there really two babies inside there?" To watch the delivery of my girls was a spectacular experience. I watched one be born, and then scrambled over with the nurses to get her cleaned up. Then I rushed back over to watch the other girl arrive. It was just a wonderful, once-in-a-lifetime experience.

I love that I got the chance to help feed my infant twins. This gave me a great opportunity I did not really have with each of our singleton boys previously. I was able to help feed my daughters every day, every night, and in the middle of the night. That was a great opportunity to hold them and bond with them, to look into their little eyes, and to hold their little hands. That's something I cherish greatly. When you get the chance to help feed your babies, and have that one-on-one time with each of them, cherish that moment because it's a spectacular joy.

Another thing to love about having twins, and I have since they were born, is that there is always somebody to hold, to hug, or to cuddle. Now that our twins are older, there is always someone to read stories to, and to play with. Even if one of the twins is having a bad day, doesn't want to talk to me, doesn't want to play with me, or is having a temper tantrum, the other twin is usually available and is eager for positive attention.

It is fun to watch your twins and how they interact with each other. This is something you don't get if you have just one baby, one infant, or one toddler. Watching my girls interact with each other has provided for a lot of entertainment, some funny moments, and fond memories. For example, if one girl is sad because she got left alone or she got hurt, the other twin will run and get the blanket of the sad sister and bring it to her, or bring a toy to her to try to comfort her. It's been fun to watch that nurturing relationship between the two of them. Whether they are at home, out in public, or at a friend's house, it is amazing to watch and observe how they care for each other.

Nothing is as quite so fun as traveling with infant twins on an airplane. (See Chapter 12 for tips on traveling with twins.) We traveled several times with our girls when they were under the age of two. I'd have one twin on my lap, my wife would have one twin on her lap, plus we'd have our two boys in their seats. It was never a dull moment on the airplane. We'd get lots of comments from people in the airport, from the flight crew, and from the passengers around us. It was always a noteworthy event to travel by plane with infant twins. Find joy in the literal journey when you are flying or driving somewhere, and enjoy how your twins are interacting with you, with their environment, with those around them.

When it came time to start our girls on solid foods, we started out with rice cereal. We put them in the booster seats in the kitchen. Then either my wife or I would sit between them. We'd scoop out little spoons of cereal and feed one twin, and then scoop up another scoop of cereal and feed the other twin, and then go back and forth between the two. The funny thing with feeding twins solids is how they would be impatient. They would both want the food at the same time. One sister would see her sibling getting the food and would reach out and try to grab the food herself, or she would start to moan, cry, or try to babble and talk to you and say that she wanted food right away. It was hilarious to watch them interact with each other and with my wife or I when we were trying to feed them solid foods. You can never feed them fast enough. You can never feed them enough. Enjoy the great memory of trying to feed them both simultaneously and when they are both covered in rice cereal. I walk you through what works great for feeding twins in Chapter 4.

Even though our twins love to do lots of things together, it's always fun to watch how different our twins can be. This is especially true as our girls are identical twins. I love watching how different their facial expressions and physical features can be, watching how their personalities diverge, and how their preferences are different. I love to pay attention to how they speak, how they pronounce their words, even the vocabulary that they use and how one of them is a little different than the other. Early on when they were learning to speak, they would call me at work to tell me something, and I would be able to identify which one of the twins I was speaking with based on her vocal intonations and mannerisms on the phone. Pay attention to the differences that you see in your twins; how they behave, how they act, how they speak, and you'll start to appreciate the beauty of how your twins can be so similar and yet so different at the same time. I talk about your twins' identity and fostering their individuality in Chapter 7.

It is always interesting to observe other people's reactions to your twins. Of course, people are going to say crazy things to you and your family when they find out that you have twins. One of the fun things is to see the people that you know, like your friends and family, start to recognize the differences in the twins, and the light bulb goes off, "I know which twin you are now!"

Having twins gives you double the opportunity to be able to be a dad and to love your kids. You get to do double tuck-ins at night, put two little kids into bed, read double the bedtime stories, sing double the bedtime songs. That's something that is amazing and awesome as a parent, to be able to have that privilege to do it twice, not just once.

I invite you today, tomorrow, and this week in your twin journey, to look for the fun moments. Look for the exciting moments. Look for the funny things that happen because you are a father of twins. It's only because you are dealing with twins that you have these things happen. Study their interactions with each other, you, their environment, friends, and family. You'll start to see that there are a lot of amazing and fun things that happen because of twins.

After the moment passes, you're going to forget those things, so try to capture them in the moment. Write them down, put them in your journal, take pictures, and take video. Share them with your wife and have her share what she experiences with you so you can capture that for your family and share with your kids as they get older. Capturing the memories you have of your twins is so important I dedicated Chapter 14 to it later in the book.

Look for the joy in the journey because it's doubly there with twins.

Essential Parenting Mindset for Surviving Infants

As you go through the day to day of raising twins, remember this simple truth:

You can't force your kids to eat, sleep, or poop. Once you learn that, life becomes a lot easier.

There is an old saying that you can lead a horse to water but you can't make him drink. Well, my friend, you've got two horses and they can often be as stubborn as mules. This book will walk you through ways of leading your twins to eat, sleep, and get on a good schedule. However, they can't be forced. You will reduce your frustration every time you remember this.

Be flexible and consistent in reinforcing the behavior you want to see and you won't have to force your kids at all — they'll do what you'd like on their own.

The road with twins will be tough. However, it can be done and survived.

If you can keep this positive mindset, it's going to be a huge benefit to you and your family, because what you're thinking is ultimately what's going to happen. If you go into the twin journey with a can-do positive attitude, it's going to make a big difference.

Tell yourself, "It's going to be hard, but I can do it. I can juggle these responsibilities effectively."

People are having twins all the time. The twins survive. Mom and dad survive, and it works out, and it will for you as well. Having a positive mindset will take it up a notch: you'll not only survive, but you will thrive.

You have to know what you're getting into. This book will paint the picture of what life will be like with your twins over the coming months. You will have conflicting commitments between work and family life (see Chapter 2). Some things are going to get squeezed. Some things are going to get dropped (just don't drop your babies). But the most important thing is that you're still able to provide for your family and take care of your twins.

As you find yourself in the throes of caring for your twins, you'll ask, "When does it start to get easier?" It doesn't happen overnight. Things get easier slowly as two things happen: your twins get older, and you get better at caring for them. They will reach milestones (which we'll talk about in this book) that make your life easier. They will also hit milestones where it seems they are regressing and your life gets harder. It is all part of the journey. The first several months are insane. Then it gets a little easier. By the year mark, you are through the fog and intensity of caring for infants. Life has reached a new normal and you're on your way!

I put together a list of twin dad affirmations that you can use to keep your mind thinking positively. Download them at www.dadsguidetotwins.com/more.

Keep reading and this book will show you how to survive and thrive as a father of twins from the time you bring your babies home through potty training and beyond.

CHAPTER TWO

Your Personal Life

As you transition to the lifestyle of being a father of twins, expect some challenges. The learning curve to twin parenting is a steep one, and everyone handles things differently.

Lifestyle changes are all about expectations — expectations you have, along with those of your family and friends. You need to try to evaluate which of your expectations are realistic and which are some that you could lower.

We found that the first year with twins was a complete blur. We know that we are not alone in this. You will be so busy just trying to keep the babies fed, changed and sleeping that all your other priorities will start to fade away or will be put on hold indefinitely.

When you do have downtime, you'll be so tired and sleep deprived that you will seek rest and relaxation above all else. This reality will mean that you find yourself choosing to cut things out of your pre-twins lifestyle that are not essential to caring for your twins.

The good news is that as your twins start to grow, your life will get easier. For example, they will start sleeping through the night, they'll start spacing out their feedings, or you can leave them with the babysitter.

You'll gradually be able to pick up some of your old habits, social events, and hobbies that you enjoyed pre-twins. The transition will be a challenge, but the really hard times are only temporary, and you'll adapt and grow and be amazed at just how much you can do with twins.

Keys to a Strong Relationship with Your Wife

Having twins and surviving the newborn months is one of the hardest things that your marriage will have to endure.

Once your twins get past the newborn phase, start sleeping through the night, and fall into a more friendly schedule, life does get back to a new normal. In that new normal, you can reestablish dating and alone time with your wife.

During the newborn months is when you have to be creative, patient, and selfless to maintain a strong relationship with your wife.

Here are some things my wife and I found successful in keeping our relationship strong despite the heavy demands of newborn twins:

- As soon as your twins start to fall into a predictable pattern of feeding and sleeping, you need to plan a date with your wife. This date may just be an hour away from the house to run an errand or go out to eat. Nevertheless, be sure to schedule this time or it will never happen. Getting a babysitter for your twins isn't too hard if you do a little prep work (see later in this chapter).
- Your wife will appreciate help when it comes time to feed the twins. Use this time to talk with your wife and stay connected emotionally. Middle of the night feedings may not be so conducive to conversation since you'll likely be sleep walking through the feeding. However, the mere act of you helping with feeding and caring for the twins will strengthen your relationship with your wife and lighten her burden.
- When the twins are sleeping, you have two options: take a nap or do something else. I typically advise that you take a nap. You'll likely be sleep deprived and need all the rest you can get.

However, you may also consider the twins' nap time as an opportunity to strengthen the relationship with your wife. Even if you are home-bound, spend time together talking, watching a movie (yes, you might fall asleep), doing chores together, etc. When the house is quiet, don't just run off to your corner to work on your projects. Spend some of that time with your wife.

- Your kids grow up and many of the challenges of feeding, sleeping, changing, and constant care fade into the past. Before it does though, talk the situation over with your wife frankly and acknowledge that this is just temporary and that any lack of attention isn't intended as a personal statement. It is simply a necessary part of this phase of parenthood.
- There will be a lack of marital intimacy after the twins are born. In due time, the physical demands of newborn twins will ease up and you can get back in your routine. Combine sleep deprivation with a wife recovering from a twin pregnancy and there will be a couple of months with not much activity in the bedroom between you and your sweetheart.
- Make conscious efforts to stay connected via touch. It can be as simple as holding hands, cuddling on the couch, and giving massages or back scratches. Patience and understanding are key during this time frame. Eventually, after your wife's doctor gives the green light, you can ease back into a bedroom routine.
- The busyness of caring for newborn twins can overshadow lots of things. It is therefore necessary to schedule and plan for time together as a couple. Try scheduling on the calendar certain nights when you'll head to the bedroom early. (Wink, wink.) No, it's not very romantic, but it will help you keep your priorities straight and help you not over-schedule yourselves with things that would distract you from each other.

Once you give up bleary eyes in favor of a full night's sleep, the world will come alive with possibilities. This will allow for more focus on your marriage.

Your marriage can and will survive newborn twins. Set clear expectations with each other. Take every opportunity to spend time together. Actively work on your relationship and it will come out stronger than ever.

Communicating with Your Partner About Raising Twins

In the newborn months and especially after you go back to work, you may worry about your wife's mental health. While it may seem that your twins are fine most of the time, you know it is stressful caring for them. Here are some things you can do to help your spouse and keep your lines of communication open and working:

Express Gratitude

Show gratitude and appreciation to your wife for all the work that she's doing to take care of your twins, what that means to you, and why it matters to you and your family.

Gratitude goes a long way to soothing the pains and the burdens that we carry. Definitely acknowledge the difficult tasks that she's been doing and the challenges she has to work through. This will make sure that she knows that she's appreciated and that it's not just a superficial sign of gratitude, but rather a deep understanding of the difficult things that she's actually doing. Acknowledge those things to her, and she'll feel better for it.

Keep Communication Open and Honest

Having open and honest communications with your spouse about your twins and family is essential to a happy home and family. Start communicating more openly today so you can get into a good rhythm of communicating.

Have open, frank, and honest discussions about your family and kids so you can quickly and easily talk through the challenges that you're facing. To put some structure around this, schedule regular weekly dates or discussions to talk about what is going on. This way you won't let things fester or drive you crazy. You have a designated time and place when you can get together and talk about issues that you are facing as a family. Discuss how you can tackle those together as a couple and as a team.

Learn Together and Plan for Parenting Success

Read good books together as husband and wife and talk about what you would want to do differently. For example, my wife and I read a parenting book together and we would try to practice one thing a day that we learned from the book during our interactions with our kids.

Find a book that may cover a topic that you're interested in, or something you would like to do with your family. Discuss and practice the concepts in that book together. This will help you work through and improve your communication with your partner so you can be the most productive, caring, and effective parents that you can be.

Remember that as you discuss things with your wife, that the amount of sleep you have been getting will affect the way you react and respond to a conversation. When you are sleep deprived, emotion starts to take more control of your thoughts and words. Acknowledge that you're going to be emotionally charged in this conversation and that you need to think through and talk through things logically with each other of how you can both meet each others' needs and the needs of your family.

Always be open and transparent in your feelings, and in your thoughts with each other. This will encourage an open dialogue between you and your spouse, so that you can be a more dynamic duo as you raise your twins.

What areas could be improved in yours and your wife's communication with each other?

FROM YOUR FELLOW PARENTS OF TWINS…

"I find it strengthened my relationship with my husband as we both tackled the twins as a team, and both developed a plan to tackle an issue. We do it as a team and we're consistent.

Everything we do or try, there is no judgment (who cares if he takes forever to bathe them and I suck at story time - we do it with no judgment from the other). Since the twins are the same age, we spend more time together as a family than if we had to separate to tackle an older/ younger child."

- *Sara Steele*

How to Give a Twin Mom a Break

Your wife has a very hard job. As a mother of twins, she is scrambling all day, every day to care for your twins – regardless of age. She deserves a break, and you know it. The question is how do you give her the break?

Frankly, there are a ton of things that you as a father of twins can do to help mom around the house with the twins. You will not get in the way, believe me. With twins there is plenty of work to do for mom *and* for dad. In fact, often there is more than both can handle.

As a father, you can always help with feeding the twins. Although it is a challenge, one person can feed two twins. Mom can breastfeed both twins at the same time, but it doesn't mean that it's easy. Whether you are breastfeeding or bottle feeding the twins in your household, you can still be of help. (See Chapter Four for specifics on how you can help with feeding the twins.)

You can take the night shift. This may work particularly well if your wife is expressing breast milk. You can bottle feed your twins either with breast milk in a bottle or with formula. This will allow mom to get a good night's rest and help her the next day as she cares for the twins – perhaps by herself if you're off to work already. Give your wife the night off and handle all the overnight baby feedings. If this is too much work (which it is in the early weeks), at least get up and help feed the twins during the night.

From the moment the twins are born until they get home (and in those early days when you're on paternity leave) take advantage of that time to see if you can change all of the twins' diapers. Yes, all the diapers. Just you, by yourself. Mom will have plenty of diapers to change soon enough.

Give your wife a break by getting out of the house and taking the twins with you. Odds are your wife has a long wish list of things she'd like to do if she had a few free moments around the house. With you and the kids gone, she'll be able to get a break and cross some things off her to-do list.

Being "trapped" at home with the twins is a surefire way to go crazy and get cabin fever. Volunteer to watch the kids while your wife goes out. Encourage her to plan a night out with friends or suggest that she run an errand by herself. Make it happen.

Get the twins dressed in the morning before you leave for work. That will make one less thing that mom needs to take care of during the day.

Give mom a break by bathing the babies. I enjoyed giving our twins baths when they were little. It gave my wife a chance to relax a little in the evening as I helped with the bedtime routine, which consisted of getting the twins in the bathtub, getting them clean, then getting them in their pajamas and ready for bed. When the twins are really young, this might be a two-person job. However, once you master the basics, you should be able to handle this responsibility yourself.

Get really good at doing the laundry. With twins, and especially newborns, there's going to be tons and tons of laundry. Be proactive in making sure that you are the one taking care of the laundry. Get the clothes washed, dried, and folded, and back into the rotation so they can be used again for your twins.

Go to the grocery store for the family or let your wife go by herself without the kids. Doing any kind of errand takes extra physical and mental effort when the twins are in tow. If you're already back to work, think about what errands you can run on the way to or from work to pick up things that you need.

There are tons of things that you can do to provide the most help to mom without feeling like you're getting in the way. And if you do feel like you're getting in the way, have a conversation. Have you asked her how can you help with the twins and around the home? It never hurts to ask. You may get a long list of things to do that you had not yet considered.

Regardless of any list you get from your wife, you need to be observant. Pay attention to what's going on around you, in your home, and with your wife and your twins.

Observe and then look for opportunities to serve. This will give you good ideas of ways to help because you have a good foundation of seeing what's happening, and then you can know where the gaps may be, or where opportunities arise where you can serve your wife and your kids.

When you're home from the office, you are on duty as a father of twins. You need to be Johnny-on-the-spot, helping everywhere and in any way that you can. This will definitely alleviate mom's burden because she will know that when you're home, you can be trusted and relied upon to assist her.

Don't assume that you know what needs to happen. Don't assume that you know what she needs. Talk to her and find out what the truth is, and then you can take action on those errands or steps or tasks that you need to do around the house to be the most helpful to her and to the babies.

You may be wondering when you'll get a break. Again, communicate that with your wife. I can promise you that as you put the needs of your family first, you will grow in love for them, and good things will come flowing back to you. Remember that this stage of your life will be relatively short. It's not the time to be selfish.

FROM YOUR FELLOW PARENTS OF TWINS…

"As a first time parent, pretty much everything that happens is a surprise, but that being said, probably my biggest surprise is not about the twins themselves but mostly regarding my wife. And it's how much energy she has, and how she can keep up with them the whole day!! That just amazes me. Basically trying to be a bit more like her is what I have been trying to change."

- Santiago Lopez

Dad's Priorities and Leaving Mom Alone with the Twins

I had to make sacrifices and changes to my personal lifestyle and to our family's lifestyle when the twins came home. That was just the reality. I did this willingly because I knew that it was not actually possible to do everything that we used to do before the twins arrived. There were not enough hours in the day and not enough hands at the house to make that possible.

I also realized that it wasn't fair to leave my wife home alone with the twins and our two older boys and for me to go off having fun and doing things as if that was not the case. Fairness aside, I didn't even see how it was physically possible for my wife to do a lot of those things alone either. Especially in those early months with twins, you need all hands on deck to help take care of the babies.

It is a father's responsibility to love and care for his family and provide for the necessities of life. This includes caring for twins even in the middle of the night and even sacrificing social activities until the twins are more self-sufficient. In the first year with twins we ended up dropping a lot of things that we used to do for fun, as a couple, or with friends – any kind of social activity, really. All those things fell off the radar, and they didn't start to pick up again until after our girls turned one.

For that first year you need to just set aside a lot of the personal things that you liked to do before and focus on the twins. It's going to be hard. It's going to be a sacrifice. You're probably not going to like it. But the reality is that's what's required, and it's one of the responsibilities of having twins.

You can slowly start to phase those things back in as the twins get older, as they start sleeping through the night, and as it gets easier to take care of them. Make sure that those are established first before you turn yourself outside the home and look for other things to do to keep yourself busy. Remember that family comes first, and it does require everybody's help at home, especially for you as the father of twins. Be involved in your family and with the twins.

FROM YOUR FELLOW PARENTS OF TWINS…

"From feeding to diaper changes to baths, there's just not enough time in the day and the days FLY by! I NEVER shower! Personal grooming has definitely taken a back seat to raising our twins. A lot of times, I'll realize it's 9 o'clock at night and I haven't even brushed my teeth!"

- Duncan Andrew McIntosh

Why Infant Twins Keep You Stuck at Home

One thing that surprised us about having twins was just how anchored to the house we were.

You'll likely feel the same way with newborn twins: stuck at home.

Why do twins create this tether to your home? Every baby has significant needs. With twins, you must take care of twice those needs plus the overhead of having two babies.

To escape the house, you'll need to get in the car. Loading up your newborn twins in the car will always take longer than you think. For example, you'll:

- Dress each twin in weather appropriate clothing (jackets, coats, etc.)
- Pack the diaper bag for all possibilities
- Load each baby in his or her car seat
- Adjust the car seat straps to account for baby's current outerwear
- Run back into the house to grab your shopping list, bag, keys, or whatever you forgot
- Stop before you've backed out of the driveway since one of your twins just had a diaper blow out
- Reverse the process to clean up the blow out mess
- Take baby back inside and clean her up
- Change her clothes (maybe yours, too) and ready her for her car seat
- Realize you need to clean the car seat, too
- Abort mission since it will take too much time to clean the seat and you can't travel without it

When you have a few trips like this, you'll start to opt for not even trying to leave the house.

Of course, it doesn't always play out like this. But even if you skip the diaper blow out, it's still a more complicated process than just you jumping in the car and taking off.

Newborn twins need to eat every couple of hours. While feedings start to spread out over time, initially, you will feel like you are constantly feeding your babies. Constant feeding doesn't offer time to leave the house. On the upside, when your twins are infants, you don't want them to be out in public much anyway. The newborns stage is your chance to chill at home.

After your twins leave the newborn stage and start taking naps a couple of times a day, you'll find that you have small windows of opportunity to get out of the house.

When the twins wake up, you'll have to feed and change them before you rush to load them up in the car, and run your errands before their next nap. You will become a pro at maximizing these windows of opportunity.

Being housebound with twins is only temporary. As your abilities as a twin parent grow, so will your ease of family excursions and errand running.

Shopping with Twins (and Toddlers)

Getting out of the house is one thing. Actually tackling a shopping trip with twins is quite another. Tack on a toddler sibling (or two) and you'll be a walking circus. Break out the popcorn and peanuts.

Ideally, both my wife and I would go shopping at the same time. That way we were able to push two carts (one of us pushed the kid cart and one of us pushed the grocery cart). This would happen after work or on the weekends when we were both available.

Alternatively, one of us would stay home with the kids, while the other one would go out to do the errands. As you know if you already have kids, going shopping and running errands usually goes a lot faster and is a lot easier when you're by yourself without kids.

Of course, both of these scenarios are the ideal, and we all know that the ideal seldom happens in real life.

If your kids are not yet able to hold their heads up or perhaps they're still in their infant carriers, then you can try putting them in the double stroller. My wife would go shopping with the inline double Snap N Go stroller. She'd push that ahead of her with one hand and then pull the shopping cart behind her with the other hand. Our two toddler boys would hold on to the Snap N Go while they walked.

Sometimes my wife would put both of the twin carriers in one cart. One carrier would snap in where a child typically sits in the basket, and the other went in the larger basket area. She would pull another cart behind her for the groceries and for the things she was purchasing. If the store wasn't too crowded, she'd let the three year old push the commodities cart while she let the two year old help her push the cart with the babies.

It made quite the visual caravan of kids when my wife was with the twins, as well as our two toddler boys who were hanging on the carts or running along behind her. The good news about shopping is that eventually the kids are going to become self-sufficient. They can walk or they can sit in the cart itself, and so this will no longer be a problem. For a season you have to make do with what you have, either having multiple carts, or using infant carriers on your person, like a sling or the Bjorn to make it easier to get around in the store.

When the girls were old enough to hold their heads up alone, a third scenario she employed was to put one girl in the seat portion of the shopping cart in her car seat (as before), she would wear the other baby in the Bjorn, and then she would have both boys walk alongside or hang on the side of the shopping cart. This was a major improvement because now there was actually some space in the shopping cart basket to put the groceries.

One of our favorite stores is Costco. The carts are so big we can actually have room for both kids to sit at the same time plus room in the basket for shopping items, but not all stores are going to be that way.

Check the type of arrangements that your favorite grocery stores have and then bring the appropriate baby carrying equipment with you, whether it's two infant carriers, a sling and a carrier, or something else.

It is important to reinforce the good and positive behavior in your twins during the shopping experience. Although they may not need it as infants, you can still practice praising them. Then when they are older, it will be easier to praise them for staying close to you, for holding on to the shopping cart, and acting appropriately in the store. You'll be able to continue that virtuous cycle of having them be well behaved in public. My wife tells me this was the key to their shopping successes, even more than creativity with the carts.

Shopping in this manner is not going to be quick or easy. We found that most other shoppers were accommodating and courteous when they realized that we had our hands full. "Better you than me," they'd often say (or a handful of other snarky comments).

You may also want to time your shopping experience during the day when most people are at work and the store is not that busy. That'll make life a little easier for you, as well. From 9:00 in the morning to 3:00 in the afternoon may be your best time window.

Don't lose hope if it takes you several tries to get out of the house and successfully do any shopping. You may have failed attempts getting everyone in the car and you'll probably want to give up. You may have times where you drive to the store and then have to head home before even getting out of the car. Other times, you may enter the store and start shopping just to have to drop what you're getting, abandon your cart, and head home — a normal scenario during potty training (more about that in Chapter 12). These are all natural and part of the challenges of taking very young twins shopping. Don't give up. You will find your groove with a good shopping routine.

From Your Fellow Parents of Twins…

"Not very long ago I headed to the grocery store with my twins. I had only an hour to do my shopping and by a miracle I only took 30 minutes, which made me an extremely happy mama.

"As I left the grocery store and started walking to our van feeling triumphant, my worst nightmare happened right before my eyes. I locked one of my twins buckled in her carseat with my diaper bag, keys and phone inside the van while holding my other twin in my arms.

"After 20 minutes of panicking and trying to calm the twin that was inside, a nice lady lent me her phone to call my husband and a policeman was able to open one window and unlock the door of the van. This experience taught me that there is goodness in the world and all around us which I am thankful for, but also taught me to be more careful and never rush.

"Joggling two energetic toddler twin girls while loading a van with groceries, holding a diaper bag and car keys is not an easy task. Life with twins is never easy but it is full funny stories like this one that did not seem funny at the moment but make you learn, remember and laugh from time to time."

- Nayelli Andrea Concha

Household Tasks That Don't Get Done With Newborns

During the early months of newborn twins, your typical household duties will fall by the wayside. There are simply more important things to worry about. Namely, mere survival.

The early days of twins is a test of the strength of your friendships. Sure, they've probably told you, "let me know if I can help." Now is the time to see if they really mean it. Here are some non-child care ideas for you to pass along to your friends who want to help:

Cleaning

With your hands full of twins, you won't have much time for cleaning your house. Your friends can come do the dishes or clean your bathrooms. Any amount of cleaning will be more than you can probably manage and will be appreciated.

Errand Running

We've talked about the Olympic feat that is leaving the house with twins. This hassle, combined with the fact that you really don't want to take your newborn twins out in public for a few weeks anyway, turns quick errands to the store into gigantic undertakings.

A friend can run to the grocery store for those few items you need and be a lifesaver.

Cooking

Unless you stocked your freezer with ready-made meals before the twins arrived, you might not be enjoying the best nutrition during the newborn twin phase. A home-cooked meal delivered by a smiling friend will make your day.

Picture Taking

It is hard to capture pictures and video of yourself with the twins if you are always the one behind the camera. Every time a friend is over visiting your home, have her take a picture of you with the twins. You'll look sleep deprived and probably ragged, but that is your reality. Document it!

Remember that your top priority is the health and well being of your twins and mom. Household chores and tasks can wait. Unfortunately, waiting also becomes an inconvenience and makes home life a little more difficult. When friends and family ask how they can help, invite them over to help around the house or run an errand for you. You'll appreciate even the simple things described above.

FROM YOUR FELLOW PARENTS OF TWINS…

"The most surprising thing has been how challenging it is to split my time and attention between three children (the twins and an older sibling). Out of necessity, I have learned to focus as much as possible on what my children seem to really need in a given moment and ignore the expectations I impose on myself for creating a certain feeling or outcome."

- Melissa Horst

How to Get a Babysitter for Your Twins

One of the great challenges in the first year or so of parenting twins is that it's hard to get out of the house without them. If this goes on too long, it directly impacts your sanity and happiness. You'll start to wonder if you and your wife will ever get to go out without kids again.

The underlying question becomes, "How long before you can go on your first date after the twins' arrival?"

The first thing you need to do is reconsider your definition of a date. With infant twins in the home, you have to start with low expectations for getting out of the house without them.

Start making your get-out-of-the-house plan when you start to see a repeatable pattern with your twins sleeping. When you put them down at night, how long do they sleep? Two to three hours is a great starting point. It's not quite long enough for dinner AND a movie but it's long enough for dinner OR a movie.

Getting a babysitter for twins is a little more complicated than with a singleton. If you still struggle with singlehandedly taking care of both your twins, then think twice about leaving them with a teenage babysitter from down the street.

Many of the dates that my wife and I took in those early days of twins started after our girls were asleep and in bed. It was much easier to have a babysitter come over and simply watch the house (and sleeping kids) than leave her with a handful of child care.

Regardless of your twins' age, a key to getting them ready for a babysitter is to have a regular bedtime routine you follow. A babysitter will be a new unknown in their space so falling back to the safety of the known routine is critical.

Also regardless of your twins' age, talk to them (repeatedly) about your date night and that you'll have a babysitter coming over to play with them and help them get ready for bed. Setting expectations early (even with very young children) will help eliminate, or at least reduce, the surprise and shock when the babysitter actually walks through the door. And just because they can't talk doesn't mean they can't understand you.

Ideally, your twins would meet the babysitter before the actual date night and in a forum where mommy and daddy are still around. Introduce your kids to the neighbor or a potential babysitter during the normal schedule you already keep. Familiarity will help comfort your twins when date night arrives.

Aside from the normal instructions you'd leave a babysitter (how to contact you, emergency info, bedtime, etc.), twins require a little extra information.

Make sure your babysitter can tell your twins apart.

Let your sitter know which blankets, toothbrushes, and other stuff goes with which child. Often your twins will know and naturally grab the right item but this isn't always the case.

Explain to your babysitter the routine your twins are used to and how that should play out in your absence.

Identify where your twins sleep and in which bed. If they are already asleep when you leave on your date, this is extra important, particularly if a given twin has special needs or is more likely to require attention.

Once you go on your first post-twins date and leave your twins at home with a prepared and competent babysitter, you'll wonder why you didn't go out sooner.

Another option you may want to consider is kid swaps with other families that you may know. In this case, you watch their kids and yours one night so the other couple can go out on a date, and then on another night, they watch your kids, along with theirs. The swapping is a little bit of extra work on your part. However, on the night that you're off, you can enjoy several hours with your wife on a date. It is a low-cost option since you don't have to pay a babysitter. And this, of course, benefits both your family and your friends.

Enjoy your evening out and don't wait too long before you go out again!

Finding a Local Group for Fathers of Twins

Fortunately for us, as fathers of twins, there are opportunities to gather together with fathers that are in the same situation as we are, typically in your local area (or even in your city or state).

There are organizations geared toward parents of multiples. These are generally groups organized and lead by mothers of multiples, but father of multiples can often piggyback on the organizations too.

There is an association at the national level called the National Organization of Mothers of Twins Clubs, or NOMOTC. This group is also called Multiples of America. The website is NOMOTC.org. On their website you're able to look up local clubs in your area by state and by city. You can find a Mothers of Multiples or a Mothers of Twins club in your city that's a part of this national association of clubs.

Even though the name says "Mothers of Twins," don't be scared away. These clubs often have subgroups within them where fathers can meet together for a dad's night out or get together as fathers for activities. These groups often welcome dads to their meetings or to their activities, so don't be too afraid to go and meet other dads of twins in your local area.

How to Find Time to Read All Those Parenting Books

As a parent you'll want to learn as much as you can about being a great parent. Reading books like this one can help you learn from others that have been in your same situation.

I understand that there often just isn't enough time to sit down and read a good book. If you want to learn something, you need to think about alternative ways to consume information.

If you've got pressing concerns about a particular topic, use the table of contents or index and just go straight to that part of the book. Reading eBooks makes this even easier because you can search for the key words or phrases that are of interest to you.

Listening to books is a great way to learn something while you are doing something else.

I love to listen to podcasts while I'm driving to and from work or even working around the house. Because I love to listen to information on the go, I started the Dad's Guide to Twins Podcast. You can find it at www.twindadpodcast.com.

I've got the Amazon Kindle App installed on my phone so I can read while I'm away from home or when I have a spare minute. Yes, this includes while in the bathroom. Don't judge; you know you do it too.

Don't expect to sit down and read full chapters of a book in one sitting. You'll likely get a page or two before you are distracted or called away to other duties. This is OK.

Unlike a riveting novel that you can't put down, reading parenting books or other nonfiction works tends to be more digestible in small chunks. I break up the books I write into smaller sections for this exact reason.

Read what you can and learn what you can even if it is just a few tidbits of knowledge at a time.

You don't have to read every book, word for word. If something doesn't apply to you or interest you, skip it. Time is precious. Only read what you'll find valuable.

You'll have lots of time where you are feeding or holding your babies. I personally mastered holding one infant cradled in my arm, holding my phone in that same hand, and bottle feeding with the other hand. This way I could continue to read (on my phone) without having to hold a big book or turn physical pages (which is difficult with one hand).

I put together a list of my favorite parenting books that have helped us as we've raised our twins. You'll find the list at www.dadsguidetotwins.com/more.

Can You Regain Your Pre-Twin Life?

It may feel like twins are a 100% time commitment. You'll feel like you've lost what you used to be and what you used to be able to do. Will you be able to return to the way life used to be before your twins arrived?

Your new reality is more family time and that's OK

The reality of having children is that you never get back to exactly the way things were before the twins were born. Twins tweak that reality even more and become the new normal for your life. This means that you need to find joy in the journey of parenting twins.

Yes, there's a lot of work and challenges with twins. However, there are also lots of fun things you can do together as a family. The older your twins get, the more mobile they become and it gets easier to go out with them to the park or other fun activities around town. Focus on the things that you can do as a family, and enjoy those moments together.

You can use the feeling of being lost and not sure of who you are to your advantage. Now is a great time to reinvent and craft yourself. You are a provider. You are a protector for your family, your kids, and your wife. You're an awesome husband, a terrific father.

What can you do to continue that pattern going forward? Be flexible and recognize that twins are a game-changer. The pattern of life will probably not return to exactly the way it was before, and that's OK. Think about what else the "new you" looks like with twins and your family situation.

What are some things that you would like to be doing that you aren't that you can start to work into your schedule and routine?

CHAPTER THREE

Work Life

Should both parents keep working after twins?

Do both parents need to work to support your family with twins?

This is a tricky question as it depends on your individual financial situation. However, there are some guidelines to help you make your decision.

Consider Child Care Costs

Child care expenses are a huge cost that will impact your decision to both return to work after maternity and paternity leaves end.

Many parents find that the cost of day care for twins is a significant portion of what one spouse was making when working outside of the home. The younger the twins, the more expensive the day care will be. Day care costs for both twins can average $15,000 - $30,000 total (or more) per year depending on where you live. That is a big price range but you can generally expect to pay more in larger cities than in smaller towns.

If one spouse is the primary money maker and his or her income could meet the needs of the family, the other spouse could stay home to care for the kids.

If more than half of one of your salaries (after taxes) is going to day care, consider staying home with your twins. Spend the time with your kids, especially when they are so young. You'll never get that time with them back. Enjoy it. You can always work later, like when the kids head off to school.

When you take child care expenses out of the picture, the day-to-day expenses of caring for twins should be covered within your regular budget. Yes, sacrifices will need to be made. However, there are many things that you don't actually need that you spend money on every month. Look for these items and focus on your true needs — not wants — and you'll see with clarity just how much income you need to support your family.

If you find that after cutting back on unnecessary expenses that you still need to have both parents working, go for it. However with some creativity, you might just be able to pay the bills, have one spouse stay at home with the kids, and avoid having to pay for day care.

Consider Desire to Work

If one or the other parent is at all a little undecided about going back to work, you may consider the question, "Do you both need to work?"

The long answer hinges on several factors: lifestyle, child care, and work effectiveness.

Seriously consider these questions and discuss them with your spouse.

Lifestyle

- What do you want your family's lifestyle to be like with twins?
- Do you want a parent to be home with the babies?

- Do you both have to work to pay the essential bills? Or do you both work to maintain a certain lifestyle?
- What would you cut back on or sacrifice in your current lifestyle if you only had one income?

Child Care

- How do you feel about others caring for and raising your children?
- How much will child care cost you? Is one of your incomes mostly going toward that expense?
- Can one parent take off at least a year or so to care for the twins?

Work Effectiveness

- Consider the demands of both of your jobs to see how accommodating they are to any potential reduced performance. Who's job would be more lenient here?
- Is it realistic to have two sleep-deprived parents working below acceptable levels?
- Could you let one parent work and help that individual get decent sleep so he or she can keep the job and perform as needed to support the family?

You have to figure out what is most important to you. Lifestyle? Money? Raising your twins yourselves? Work?

You both may feel that two incomes are needed just to provide for your new offspring. This may or may not be the case, depending on your priorities.

To help aid your decision, you can download a worksheet that will walk you through these questions. Get the worksheet at www.dadsguidetotwins.com/more.

Twins require sacrifice of almost everything you currently take for granted, income included. Consider your situation from all angles before you make a united decision. Unity is ultimately what will make your decision successful.

How Do Twins Impact Work Life?

As a father of twins, one of my major concerns is providing for my family. This, of course, requires work.

The reality of having twins is that they will impact your work life.

Suddenly having two new mouths to feed is by itself a great motivation to make the money necessary to provide and care for your twins.

At the time our girls were born, I looked at my job with a new perspective. I wanted to make sure it was secure and that I performed well enough to earn the necessary wages for my family.

The good news is that your financial motivations will push you to work even when your body is dragging from the reality of caring for twins at home.

With infant twins in the home, you will be called upon to care for them during the night. While you feed, change diapers, and soothe crying babies, you are missing out on the sleep you need to properly function during the day.

Depending on your parenting methods and the development and personalities of your twins, they could be sleeping through the night as early as 2-3 months old. However, it's not uncommon for parents to find their children still waking during the night well into toddlerhood. Be prepared for the long haul and celebrate when you start getting a full night's sleep again.

Sleep Deprivation and Its Impact on Your Efficiency at Work

You'll think less clearly. You'll be slower in reacting to questions or issues. You'll forget things more easily. You won't be able to do as much as you used to. Take extra care as you drive. My dad is a sleep specialist and would often remind me that driving sleepy is as dangerous as driving drunk.

Set expectations with your boss and coworkers that this is your temporary reality. Plan ahead and give yourself extra time for tasks and projects.

During the early months with twins, they will have countless checkups and doctor visits. These visits will go a lot smoother if you can help your spouse. Since doctors typically see patients only during business hours, if you want to go with your twins, you'll need to get time off work to help.

We tried to arrange appointments for first thing in the morning, during lunch, or at the end of the day so it would be easier for me to get away from the office and help.

If you run your own business or work from home, twins become an even greater challenge. Since you'll be in the home with your twins, you will be "available" to help even if you are supposed to be working and not interrupted.

If you aren't able to get everything done, you might need to get out of the house to remove distractions. You may need to alter your work schedule. Try packing in work during nap times. You can even do business one-handed on your phone while you bottle-feed a baby with the other hand.

Balancing Work and Family Life

There are other ways that you can manage working and spending time with your children. You may want to consider how your work schedule is structured. Are you able to go to work earlier in the day so that you can get home earlier to spend time with your family? If it's possible, reserve the weekends for dedicated family time. Try to get the work done that you have during the week so you don't have to bring it home with you on the weekends.

Don't get so caught up working that you miss out on the time you can spend with your twins. Working from home is a great advantage in that you can see them and spend time with them while everyone else is away at an office.

If your business or work depends on your top performance, your business will suffer during the first year with twins. Unfortunately, this is the reality of the demands twins bring when they arrive in your family.

The good news is that it doesn't last forever. You can plow through the challenges of the early months and adapt to the new reality of parenting twins. Your work life will return to a new normal and the constant motivation of caring and providing for your twins and family will help you get creative in working effectively.

Taking a Promotion vs. Family Life with Twins

Balancing the responsibility to provide for our families and being there to help raise and care for them is a great challenge for any father. What should you do if you have a promotion coming up at work and it will require more time away from home?

Ask: will a promotion help offset any lost wages from your wife staying home with the kids? If you need that money to survive, you should take the promotion. If the money isn't an issue, perhaps because the raise with the promotion isn't that big, or you've already got what you need saved up, then a promotion at this time may not be the best fit for your family. This is especially true if it will require more time away from your home. While your twins are infants, you can be a lot of help at home with your kids.

If you pass up a promotion, think about how that impacts your future career. Will the opportunity arise again? Could you transfer to another location or company and get the promotion later? If you don't have to take the promotion now, consider that option. Consider deferring that for later so you can focus on your family right now. Think about how much time you'll have at home to help with the twins. The most intense time with twins is during the infant months and the first year. It is possible for your wife to handle the twins by herself, but it will be very difficult, completely exhausting, and wearing on her.

This decision is not easy. However, you can find the balance between work and family. In the case of a big promotion, it may require calling in extra help on the family front to help with the twins, deferring the promotion, or declining it. Do what you feel is best for your family.

How to Mentally Transition from Work to Home

The transition from work to home is very important to prevent the stress and burdens of work from creeping into home life.

Look for small things that you can do to help ease the transition to home life. This could be an extra drive around the block as you approach your home, or maybe even walking to go get the mail at the mailbox. It may be something you can do around the home before you enter the house like taking in the trashcans or pulling some weeds. Find something that will help you mentally transition into family life.

You may have only a few minutes to transition, but you need to make the most of them. Evaluate what you do in your car for the commute home, and see if there's something else that can help you get ready to put your dad hat on. Maybe use the drive time to mentally prepare for that transition, to think about what's going to be waiting for you when you get home.

Perhaps change what you're listening to on the radio if good music will help you get pumped up to jump into the fray. Or turn the radio off completely so that you can focus on this mental transition. If you have a good friend you can chat with on a hands-free headset on your way home to help you relax, do it. Or when you arrive home, spend a few moments in the driveway or in the garage meditating before you enter the house.

Even if you can find just a few minutes of transition and do a little extra to mentally prepare yourself before you enter the home, it's going to be a big, big relief and make things easier for everyone, you included, when you go in.

Don't let animosity build up that you don't get a break. Odds are, mom has been home with the kids all day and she hasn't had a break either. **Plan breaks for each other to take. Remember that**

caring for mom and dad is actually a big part of caring for twins.

Once you open the door, there will likely be screaming, diapers to change, and a frazzled wife to hug, but enjoy a moment. Find a moment that's positive and happy and focus on that. Perhaps it's holding one of your babies or seeing the smile of one of your twins. It'll help you focus on the positive and not all the chaos that is in a twin household.

I find that when coming home from work, I do have to jump right into domestic challenges and I don't get a break, often until the kids are in bed. If you're not able to find time to relax between work and home, plan for some down time a little later in the evening, so that way you'll have something to look forward to and you have a light at the end of the tunnel after the kids go to bed.

Handling Guilt of Leaving Mom Home Alone with Twins

As a working dad, you'll have some guilt of working outside the home, even at nights, and leaving the twins (and other kids, if you have them) alone with your wife.

Remember that we each have a role to play in the home. This includes dad, mom, and the kids. Don't feel too guilty because you are fulfilling your role. Your role here is working to provide for your family. Your wife, in this case, is staying at home to take care of the kids.

I work so that my wife can stay home and teach and care for our children. One way to help reduce the guilt is to make sure that you're not leaving a heavy burden for your wife at home. You can do this by preparing everything that your wife needs in your absence so that she's not scrambling or extra stressed while you're away.

Remember, when you are home, that you need to be engaged and paying attention to your family, twins, and wife. You need to be fully plugged in to activities, chores, and household responsibilities. That means you're going to need to turn off your computer, cell phone, video games, and television. Focus on your wife and kids when you are home.

This will help your relationship with your wife and your children. If they know that when daddy is home, things will be good, it will help reduce your guilt when you have to be away at work.

Relationship with Twins When Away from Home

You may have a career that requires you be away from home. This could be frequent business travel or overseas military deployment. In these cases, how do you give good support to your wife and twins while you're far away?

The first key to success is that you want to be part of your family's life, and you want to be involved, even from a distance. This mindset will ensure that you keep your wife and your kids in the front of your mind while you are away, and that you'll take advantage of opportunities to talk with them.

When your twins are very young, connecting with them via video will be a great way for you to stay familiar and be a part of their lives while you are away. Probably due to time zone differences between where they live and where you'll be, you might not always be able to chat at the same time of day, or while the whole family is awake. However, your wife could show your twins a video of daddy singing a good night song or reading a story as part of their bedtime ritual. Try to continue some routine that you may have with them now by doing recordings that your twins can see on a daily basis while you're away.

You may also consider writing regular, personal letters to each of your twins while you are away. They won't necessarily understand them now, because they're so young. But they will be very meaningful as your twins grow older and you can review and discuss them together.

CHAPTER FOUR

Feeding

Although this chapter is titled "Feeding," you'll notice that we talk a lot about sleep. In the early days and weeks of twins, it's hard to separate the two. As you read through this chapter, you'll notice a gradual separation. Your life with twins will mirror this experience.

As with many things and your twins, feeding requires a key mindset: be flexible. You'll try many different techniques, schedules, foods, and patterns before you find your rhythm and what works.

Just when you get a handle on something that works, your twins will change and you'll need to reinvent yourself. This is part of the feeding game with twins. Not only do you have the normal infant logistics of feeding, but you have the logistics of handling both babies at the same time.

Newborn Twins Feeding Schedule

Twins and their feeding needs will require you to be flexible (day or night) to accommodate their feedings.

Sometimes parents get a lucky break when their babies sleep through the night, but don't count on this happening right away or when you really want it to.

When one twin seems like they could sleep through the night, the other wakes up and starts crying. This inevitability leads to two hungry and crying newborns. A good rule of thumb is that newborns need to be fed every 2 – 3 hours.

Newborn Twins Feeding Schedule for the First Month

For the first week, twins will sleep for 14 – 18 hours per day. In the following weeks, twins are expected to sleep between 12 – 18 hours per day. These numbers sound great, but there is a downside. They will only sleep for 2 – 3 hours at a time. When they wake up, they will want to be fed.

I recommend that when one twin wakes up, you wake the other and you feed both twins at the same time. Keeping your twins on the same schedule will make your life a lot easier and will drastically shorten the amount of feeding time.

One parent doesn't have to do all the nighttime feedings. Both parents can wake up and care for the newborns or you can take turns with a helper for the overnight duties. Just about the time you get used to a routine, your twins will change things. So don't get too comfortable (although sleeping for 2-3 hours at a time isn't too comfortable to begin with!).

Newborn Twins Feeding Schedule after Six Weeks

Twins will go through cycles and each pair is different. Some will find their schedules right away, while others will take longer to settle into a routine. Typically, the hectic schedule of the first month will taper off when the newborns are around six weeks old. This is right around the time when you will notice that they start to sleep for longer periods of time. Over the next few months, twins will eventually start to sleep for 4 – 6 hours at a time. This makes feeding times much easier because you will finally be able to sleep for more than a few hours. However, even with the twins' feeding schedule changing, expect to still need to feed your twins one to two times per night.

Sleep deprivation and a crazy first year are the reality of every twin parent. Thankfully, twins will start sleeping more as they grow older and this definitely helps your health and well being. Once twins start eating in larger amounts, feeding them every few hours can be changed. By the time they are about six months old, most twins will be eating four times a day. This, of course, is determined by their weight and health.

If you are ever in doubt of how much and how frequently your twins should be eating, please consult your pediatrician.

FROM YOUR FELLOW PARENTS OF TWINS…

"During the first 2 weeks, had to force-feed the twins every two hours to get rid of jaundice. All the girls wanted to do was sleep! They'd fall sleep mid-feed. We tried everything to keep them awake (sing, change diapers, and take off their clothes). Finally, my husband grabbed the spray bottle we used to keep the cats away and started spraying our daughters' heads with water every time they nodded off to sleep, then quickly jam the bottles in their mouths to get them to angrily eat. After three straight all-nighters, absolutely no judgment here and we both started laughing!"

- *Sara Steele*

Framework for Twin Sleeping and Feeding Schedules

You can create a framework that encompasses both sleeping and feeding schedules for the twins. It's going to take some work on your part.

As an overarching theme, keep your twins on the same schedule. Your activities and efforts should be focused on getting your twins aligned on the same schedule, and it will make your life a lot easier. I really like the framework that is outlined in the book, "Secrets of the Baby Whisperer: How to Calm, Connect, and Communicate with Your Baby" by Tracy Hogg. She has a formula called the "EASY formula" that we used with our girls with great success.

The gist of the EASY formula is that your babies are going to go through a cycle. E is for eating. A is for activity. S is for sleep. Y is for you; for your time. So, your babies should go through this cycle multiple times a day, and the time between the different steps in the formula will change over time as your babies get older. But the pattern is the same. You're going to feed your babies. They're going to have some kind of activity, either playing with you or tummy time, and then they're going to go to sleep. Of course when they're sleeping it's time for you to take a break and catch up on the things that you have to do. We found this pattern (and Tracy Hogg's book) very valuable not just with our twins, but our singleton babies as well.

If your twins are your induction to parenthood, please trust me when I tell you that this formula is a lifesaver. When you know exactly where you are in the cycle, you more quickly learn to differentiate your twins' cries of hunger from cries of discomfort from cries of being tired. You will save yourself lots of frustration when you are so tired you can't think straight but you have these two crying babies to deal with.

The last virtue I want to extol about the EASY formula is that right from the start, there is time built in for self-care. Let this be the pattern for your parenting and always take some time for you. You will not be effective at anything you need to do if your resources are depleted.

Feeding Both Twins at the Same Time

If you want to keep your twins on the same schedule it will require you to overcome some logistical challenges of handling both twins at the same time.

For example, if one of your twins is a good eater and the other is a fussy eater, you'll need to adapt. Each twin may react differently to their feeding. Burps and the rhythm of feeding vary with each child.

To overcome these challenges, you'll have to take turns, as there isn't really another way when they both require special attention. Most of the time when the twins are being cooperative, you can feed them both at the same time. However, when they're off their game a little and one needs more attention than the other, you're going to have to switch your attention and focus on each of them one at a time.

Feeding Logistics

One thing that we liked to do when we were bottle-feeding our girls is that one of us, my wife or myself, would sit on the floor between two bouncy seats and pop a bottle in each baby's mouth to feed them. This worked great when they were happy and drinking, but sometimes one of them gets fussy, one needs a burp, and you just have to stop feeding them and take care of that one infant at that time.

Keep in mind they'll likely cry when they're not getting food and attention. That's natural, and it's okay, and it's not the end of the world.

You don't need to get stressed, you don't need to freak out, and you don't need to rush more than is needful in this situation. Hang in there, take a deep breath, and switch back and forth between the two babies. Even from a very early age, this is going to teach your twins that they're not the only one who needs attention and that they will have to share lots of things, including your attention.

Remember that it's always okay — whether while feeding or in other cases like changing diapers, getting dressed, helping potty train, you name it — it's always okay to take care of one twin at a time.

Should you wake twins at the same time for feeding?

Caring for infant twins overnight is a very demanding and exhausting responsibility. You want to take care of their needs as quickly as possible and then get them (and you) back to sleep.

Should you wake up your twins at the same time for nighttime feedings? Most of the time, I'd say "yes." In actuality, the answer is "it depends."

As with many aspects of caring for your twins, your situation varies each day. It is thus extremely important that you stay flexible in how you attend to your babies.

My general rule of thumb is that when one twin wakes up in the middle of the night and is ready to eat, you should wake up the other and feed them both.

When our girls were infants, we followed exactly this pattern. When one of our daughters woke up hungry, my wife and I would get out of bed and head into the nursery. One of us would take the crier, and the other would wake up the sibling.

We'd feed both babies, burp them, change them, and put them back to bed. We could then zombie walk back to our own beds and sleep until we heard the next set of cries.

The twins stayed on a relatively predictable (and nearly identical) schedule. This allowed us to get at least some rest at night between feedings that would have been truncated if we fed each twin one after the other.

If your twins are breast fed, it will be more of a logistical challenge to position and feed both babies at the same time. However, it is possible and you should try and stick to the "one wakes up, they both eat" nighttime schedule.

When your twins start to take turns eating, it makes for a very long night for mom, dad, or the caregiver. By the time you feed both babies, one at a time, burp them, change them, and get them back to bed, there is very little time for you to sleep before it starts all over again.

So, should you wake up your twins at the same time to feed them? Yes, if you want to maximize your sleep and keep some sanity to your already crazy, sleep-deprived schedule.

FROM YOUR FELLOW PARENTS OF TWINS…

"I really expected the sleep deprivation to be a lot worse. But once we got out of the 'feeding every few hours stage' and put them on a fairly strict schedule, things weren't that bad. We had my girls sleeping through the night by two months old. So we decided to go ahead and move them to their own cribs way sooner than we expected. I was never much of a schedule person before but now I love them."

- Zachary Head

Should You Have Staggered Feedings with Twins?

Although I have advocated for keeping your twins on the same schedule, you might ask, should I have staggered feedings with twins? The answer to this question lies in what will work best for your family, your schedule, and your sanity.

When we talk about staggered feedings, I mean that you feed one twin, burp, diaper them, and then feed the other twin.

During the first 4-6 weeks, when the babies will be eating every 2-3 hours, there will not be a lot of time for you to catch a break if you stagger feed. It will seem to the person taking care of the feeding that they are always feeding somebody.

Even as they get older and start to space their feeding needs out a little more, you or your wife could run yourselves ragged on a staggered schedule. Remember the EASY formula? With the staggered feeding schedule, it looks more like Eat (E), Activity (A),

Sleep (S), E, A, S, E, A, S, E, A, S… Guess how long you'll last? There's little or no time for you.

You should consider stagger feeding if your babies are efficient eaters. Our oldest son (singleton) was a "sitcom baby," meaning my wife could sit down to nurse him and watch an entire sitcom episode before he was done nursing. Our second son (also a singleton) could nurse in six minutes flat and be done. If your twins are efficient like this, it won't matter much if you stagger feed.

The big advantage of staggered feedings for your twins is that one person can handle all the feedings. This advantage is not to be undervalued. Especially if one parent is home alone with the twins, this might be the only option to keep both sanity and the kids fed.

If tandem breast-feeding of your twins isn't working, staggering the feedings will be easier.

The good news is that you can change your mind if a schedule isn't working. Try something and if you realize it just isn't going to work, be flexible and adapt. Twins require creativity and quick adaptation. Feeding schedules are no exception.

Preparing Bottles for Twins

After unsuccessfully trying to breastfeed our newborn twins, we moved to bottle-feeding. At first my wife pumped and we filled bottles with breast milk. After several weeks of this, we switched to formula feeding.

Finding the right formula

There are three types of baby formula: ready to use, powdered, and concentrate. When you get free or cheap formula direct from the manufacturer, you can't always pick what type of formula you want. We preferred the powdered kind because you didn't need to refrigerate it after it was opened.

You'll need to experiment with which brand of formula works best for your twins. We had success with bulk formula from Costco since it was cost effective, and our girls consumed it just fine.

How Many Bottles?

Your twins will go through between 6 and 8 bottles per day per baby. You can stock that many bottles in your home or just be prepared to wash them throughout the day.

You'll typically find different types of bottles for your twins at the store.

Bottles come in various sizes: 4 oz., 8 oz., 9 oz., 11 oz., etc. If you want to save money, buy a larger size. You'll need it eventually, and you can still use it for newborns with the right nipple and without filling it up all the way.

Temperature Control

Make sure you don't give your babies scalding hot formula or milk to drink.

The microwave is notorious for unevenly heating liquids and can give your baby an unpleasant surprise.

When we had to reheat breast milk that was stored in the freezer, we'd warm a large cup of water in the microwave, then take that out and let the bag of milk sit in the water for a few minutes to warm up. This gave us a more even warming without any super-hot surprises.

For formula, we kept a pitcher of water on the counter at room temperature that we used for mixing up the formula. Room temperature water worked great and our girls did fine with it.

Preparing the Bottles

You'll get so good at preparing bottles that you'll be able to hold one baby with one arm and make a bottle with the other.

One of the tasks that my wife or I would take care of during downtime was preparing bottles for the next feeding. We'd scoop the desired amount of formula into a clean bottle and set it on the counter next to a clean nipple, ring, and the room temperature bottle of water. Then we'd quickly hand wash the dirty bottles so they'd be ready to use later.

When it came time to feed, we just added the right amount of water, screwed on the nipple, shook the bottle up, and then sat down to feed the twins.

Getting all the bottles prepared ahead of time will make life a lot easier when one parent is home alone with the twins. Plus getting everything in order before bed helps you avoid any mistakes that tend to be really easy to make in the middle of the night.

How to Single-Handedly Bottle Feed Infant Twins

Once you've decided to bottle feed your infant twins (with either formula or breast milk), you'll need to figure out *how* to conquer the logistics of feeding two babies by yourself.

Help Holding the Babies

Use nursing pillows to support your babies during feeding.

Place each twin in their own nursing pillow with the pillow supporting their head, neck, and upper back and their bodies resting in the U-space of the pillow. Sit down on the floor or your bed, put a twin on either side of you, and hold the bottles for your hungry babies. Don't forget to use something to support your back or else the feeding will become excruciatingly long.

Another variation is similar to the nursing pillow but uses bouncy seats. We most often used two bouncy seats that we'd lay each girl in at an incline. We'd have them a few feet apart, both facing the same direction. My wife or I could then sit between them on the ground, with our back against the sofa, facing the twins.

Use bouncy seats to hold your twins for feeding time.

We'd then hold one bottle with each hand and feed the girls at the same time. Make sure you have some arm support, like a pillow or find a way to rest on the bouncy seat, otherwise, you'll get really tired, really fast.

Burping Infants

As each twin is different, you'll find that your babies need to be burped at different times when you have others helping you or at the same time when you are by yourself.

It is OK to stop feeding both when one needs to be burped. The other twin will cry, but it isn't the end of the world. You'll become the master of quickly burping one baby so you can move on to the next.

When feeding twins by yourself, you will find that spit ups happen because you couldn't burp them fast enough. It is messy. It is extra work to clean up. It is totally natural. Remember that you are doing the best you can.

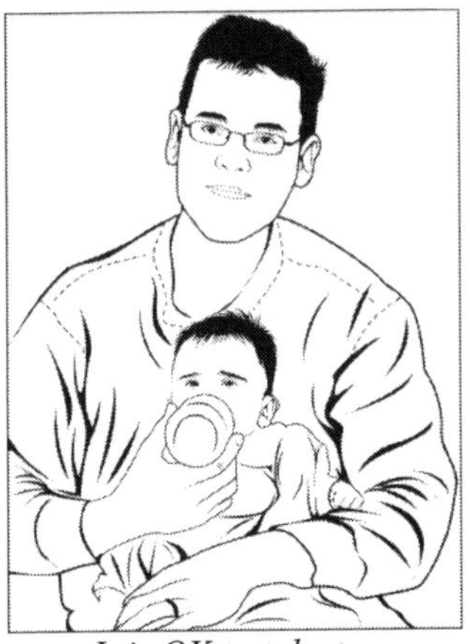

It is OK to take turns.

You don't have to feed your twins at the same exact time. If you must, take turns. Remember that one secret to your sanity is to handle each twin one at a time. Staggered feedings are a valid option when it is only you taking care of the twins.

Get Helpers

Don't assume that you have to do everything by yourself. When you can, use helpers.

My wife and I found it easiest to each hold and feed a baby whenever I was home. Of course, this means you need two adults to feed two babies. This will only work for you if you have another set of helping hands at home.

I highly recommend that you recruit some helpers (family, friends, etc.) to help you through the first year of twins. Whether it's as simple as having a friend come over and help with the daytime feeding, or as complex as finding live-in help, you will be grateful to have others to make your load lighter.

An extra pair of helping hands is always welcome.

Once your twins are sitting up and starting to crawl, they may not be interested in their bouncy seats anymore. By this point, it is also easier to lift and position them, so try sitting them on each of your legs, their back to your front. As they cuddle into you, pop the bottles in their mouths. Not only do you get cuddle time, but now your arms don't lose feeling by the end of a feed.

Once they can sit up by themselves, it is easier to feed both at the same time.

How you feed your twins, where they eat, who feeds them, and the timing of everything doesn't really matter. The most important thing is that your twins do eat and get the nourishment they need to thrive and grow.

Try different methods and styles to see what works best for you and your family.

Eventually they can feed themselves!

You won't be holding bottles out at arms' length forever. The twins will eventually be able to hold their own bottles, which my wife tells me was one of the happiest days of her life.

Twin Discounts on Formula

The costs of formula feeding your twins can add up rather quickly. To help ease the financial burden, you'll need to get some twin discounts on formula. With some proper sleuth work and some trusty advice from the pediatrician, you should be able to save some money and still get your babes the nutrition they need.

While at the hospital, the nursing staff supplemented my wife's breast milk with formula to keep our twins well fed.

When we left for home, our nurses gave us several containers of baby formula to take with us. These were all single serving size containers but worked great for us. The formula from the hospital came in handy when feeding our girls at home.

Before you leave the hospital, ask your nurses for extra formula and other supplies that you can have. Remember: it never hurts to ask! It will work to your advantage to treat your nurses kindly and show gratitude for their help.

Some pediatricians will give you a free bottle of formula (or more) if they have it in stock. Ask every time you go for your well-baby checkups with the twins.

In addition, your pediatrician will have information about twin discounts on formula directly from manufacturers. We picked up a few forms from our doctor that we filled out and mailed in to the companies. This effort resulted in free baby formula shipped to our house. One shipment was liquid formula that was a little different from the powdered version we were using, but it is hard to turn down "free" formula.

Costco and other similar warehouse style stores sell big volumes of formula at a discounted rate.

Ask your medical professionals, reach out to manufacturers, shop wisely, and you'll never have to pay full price on baby formula.

You'll find a list of formula manufacturers and discount options at www.dadsguidetotwins.com/more.

Breastfeeding Twins

As a father, you won't be breastfeeding your twins any time soon, because, well, that's just nature's way.

However, many mothers of twins choose to and successfully have breastfed babies.

Before our twins were born, my wife planned on breastfeeding them. She had successfully breastfed their older brothers and wanted the same experience for our twins.

The reality of breastfeeding twins quickly forced us to change our feeding pattern. We had to do not only what was best for our babies, but for the entire family.

In our case, our girls couldn't get a good latch to breastfeed effectively. They had short frenulums and this led to babies not getting enough food and struggling through each feed. My wife tried patiently to work through this with each baby but the deal breaker was the older siblings. Our 3 year old and 22 month old still required quite a bit of attention and would do naughty things as soon as my wife sat down to work with one of the infant girls. Between the girls not getting enough while nursing and their attention-deficit brothers, it quickly became apparent that bottle-feeding would be best for the entire family.

There are many moms that successfully breastfeed their twins and you can, too. Just remember to be open to what works for your family and twins and be prepared to change course if needed.

Talk with a lactation consultant. This is a specialist that can help teach mom the proper methods of feeding babies. You can ask to see a lactation consultant while still in the hospital after the twins are born. Alternatively, you can ask your pediatrician for a recommendation. After the birth of our first son, we had a lactation consultant come to our home to help get us on the right track.

If you or your wife are feeling frustrated that breastfeeding isn't going well, don't assume you have to figure it all out by yourself. Seek out a lactation consultant.

As your wife and twins learn how this whole breastfeeding thing works, it is perfectly fine to supplement with formula. This will take the pressure off and give you time to figure out the mechanics of breastfeeding without worrying about if they are getting enough nutrition.

Mom and babies will need to practice different positions to see what works best. A traditional position is a double football hold where mom holds the head of each baby in each of her hands. The babies' bodies then are tucked under her arms.

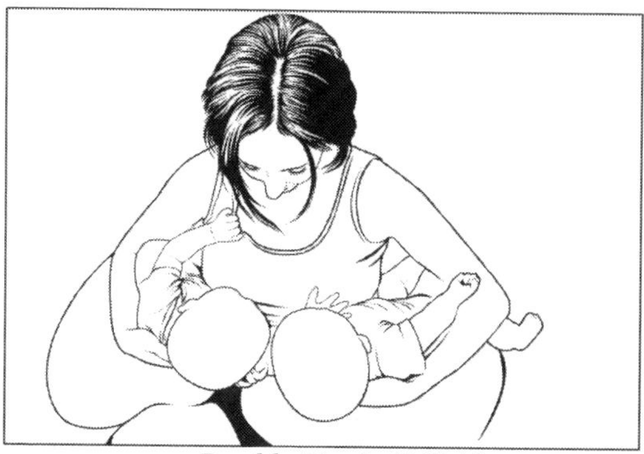

Double Football Hold

Another option is where mom lies flat or reclined on her back with the babies' heads on mom's breasts and their bodies laying down towards her lap. The babies may crisscross over each other or not.

Crisscross or V-Position

A third position that might work well for your babies is feeding them in a parallel position. Baby A has her head on mom's breast and her body sits on mom's lap. Baby B is on the other breast and her body and legs point off the side such that both babies are pointing their legs in the same direction.

Parallel Feeding

You'll need to experiment with different positions to see what is comfortable for mom and works for the babies.

You, dad, need to help with the logistics surrounding breast-feeding. You can help bring babies to mom. You can help position them in the right spots. You can burp and change the babies when they are done with feedings.

Additionally, you can help stock and supply all the baby gear needed to support breastfeeding. Despite what it looks like on the outside, breastfeeding can really hurt mom. She'll get very tender breasts and nipples that might even crack and bleed if not cared for properly. You can help relieve her pain and burden by making sure you have the right tools in place.

Lanolin works great for soothing sore nipples. Your wife will also benefit from heating pads for relaxing her tender breasts.

Get a high quality breast pump so mom can store up some milk in the freezer for later feedings. This will let you help bottle feed the twins in the middle of the night. Or (gasp!) even go out on a date with your wife and leave the babies at home.

Breastfeeding isn't easy but it is a great way for babies to get top quality nourishment and bond with mom. You need to do all in your power to help mom be successful with this endeavor.

Since the burden is really on mom for this method of feeding, you need to support her decision. If she wants to drop breastfeeding in favor of bottles, go for it. If she wants to press ahead with breastfeeding, support her in that decision, too.

How to Help Your Wife Feed the Twins

Even though feeding time with twins can get crazy, I enjoyed the opportunity to help feed my infant daughters. With our previous singleton births, my wife was able to handle the feeding and I never really got to participate. With twins, the extra work necessitated my help, and it was a rewarding experience to be able to hold my daughters and feed them (yes, even in the middle of the night).

How can you help your wife feed the twins?

It depends on how you'll be feeding them. Will your wife be breast-feeding the babies or will you be bottle-feeding formula to your twins?

Breast-Feeding

Consider all the steps required to breast-feed your twins simultaneously. Here is a simplified list:

1. Get seated
2. Position the pillow(s) to support the babies
3. Pick up and position one baby on one side
4. Pick up the other baby and position her on the other side
5. Get baby #1 to latch and start feeding
6. Get baby #2 to latch and start feeding
7. When baby #1 finishes, mop up any spills and help burp
8. When baby #2 finishes, mop up any spills and help burp
9. Return babies to original location (crib, blanket on floor, etc.)

Sorry, dad, you won't be able to breast-feed your babies. However, in this case you will play a critical supporting role. As you'll notice in the list above, many of the steps can be handled by you. You can help bring the twins to your wife and get them positioned. You can help clean up and burp your babies. And you even get diaper duty.

Ideally, your wife would breast-feed the twins simultaneously. If not, then she will need your help with the twin she's not feeding while she nurses the other.

If for some reason your babies aren't able to breast-feed directly, your wife may end up pumping breast milk that can then be bottle-fed to your babies. There will be greater opportunity to help here as well.

Bottle-Feeding

Whether your babies are drinking breast milk or formula from a bottle, the logistics of feeding are almost identical.

The big difference is in the preparation of the bottles. Formula may be a powder that needs to be mixed up. Breast milk may come out of the freezer and need to be warmed up first.

Whenever I was home and it was time for the babies to eat, each adult fed one baby. If you are able to mimic this same pattern, you as the father will be able to easily help your wife. You can prepare the bottles and feed a baby while she helps with the other.

What Happens With the Other Kids?

When you have other kids in the house, things get complicated. They will need attention during almost every feeding, except perhaps the middle-of-the-night feeds.

In these cases, your responsibility may be to take care of the sibling(s) instead of directly helping with feeding the twins. When you remove the burden of the other children from the person feeding the twins, feeding time becomes a little easier. In Chapter 10, I talk in more depth about handling your other kids with twins at home.

You Can Help Feed Your Twins

Even though dads aren't built to directly feed babies, you can still be a great help and assistance to your wife regardless of what your babies are eating. Talk through feeding options with your wife and clearly state how you want to help. If you leave the decision to the last minute, when the babies are crying in the middle of the night, you won't be able to make a clear decision. Decide now how you want to feed your babies and what your role will be in the feeding process.

Bottle Feeding Twins: Middle of the Night Tips

If you choose to bottle feed your twin babies, you'll face the challenge of making bottles in the middle of the night.

The middle of the night feeds are generally heralded when one of your babies starts crying. This jars you from your slumber and pulls you out of your warm bed. You may even find yourself sitting on the edge of your bed trying to figure out what is the next thing you are supposed to do.

Because of the bewildered stupor that you will likely experience during night feedings, you need to have everything ready before you go to bed.

Before you go to bed, lay out burp cloths, bottles, formula, and a container of water.

When your babies start crying for food, they want food and they want it now. The longer you take, the louder the cries and the more frustrated you will get, especially when you're sleepy.

We'd have bottles and nipples ready on the kitchen counter next to the formula canister and the feeding log. The bottles would have the water already pre-measured and ready to add the formula. Dump, shake, and go!

For water, we filled up a Tupperware-style water bottle with a flip top lid and kept it on the counter. The big advantage of this was that the bottle was always room temperature and ready for immediately feeding the baby. No, your babies don't need warm milk, so save yourself some time and frustration by going the room temperature route.

As with many things when it comes to twins, you'll find yourself making choices–and sacrifices–constantly. In this case, you'll probably weigh the benefits of being organized (especially if it doesn't come naturally) against a few minutes of extra sleep. Do yourself a favor, prepare when you are awake so you can sleep walk through the process quickly and then quickly return to bed.

FROM YOUR FELLOW PARENTS OF TWINS…

"One of the funniest moments (after the fact) was a early morning feeding at around 2am. My wife and I were barely awake and Sean was crying very hard. So I rushed and get a bottle ready. Then for some reason I didn't put the nipple on. I instead handed the bottle and nipple to my wife, who then proceeded to give it straight to Sean. However with no nipple, the formula went all over Sean. The poor kid was drenched. We had to change all his clothes and make a new bottle up. We both had a good laugh the next day."

- Michael L. Sylvester

Nighttime Feedings When Twins Are Not in Your Room

If you decide to arrange things such that your twins sleep in their own room, then the sky's the limit on how you can take care of them during the night and how you decide to feed them.

We put our girls in their own room right after we got home from the hospital. When it was time for nighttime feedings, my wife would take one girl and I would take the other. We'd stumble into the kitchen and one-handedly prepare the bottles of formula, and then we'd go into the family room, in our sleepy trance, and we'd feed them.

We had a night-light on the stove in the kitchen to help us with the bottle preparation.

Keep all the lights off while feeding so that the twins stay sleepy and easily go back to sleep after you're done.

If your twins are not in the same room with you, try taking them to a common room, like the family room. Or you can even feed them in their room, if you want to, if you have the furniture to support that. Odds are, you may have just a single rocking chair in your babies' room, and so it may be easier, if both parents are helping with the feedings in the middle of the night, to take them out to a bigger room where there's more seating for the adults.

Types of Bottles for Twins

Which types of bottles will be best for you? There are several different options to consider.

Hands Free Bottles

Hands Free bottles are a clever invention that makes feeding time easier. Models like the Podee Baby Bottle make it easy for your twins to drink without having to hold up the heavy bottle.

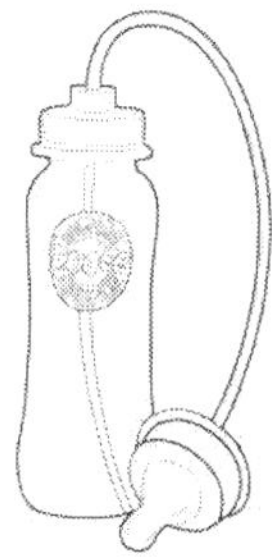

Podee Bottle

This hands free bottle works great for parents of twins. You will be able to hold both of your babies at the same time since you don't need to hold the bottle. Or you can hold one baby for one feeding and let the other be held on the next feeding. We didn't know about this neat invention when we were feeding babies, so I can't speak to this from personal experience, but the theory sounds great.

This type of bottle is also great if you have things you need to get accomplished or are on the go. If you are doing a chore or errand you might find it extremely difficult to be able to hold and feed your child while also getting your daily activities accomplished. Remember that while these types of bottles help your twins feed more easily, they still need help and supervision!

Consider All Types of Bottles

There are many other types of bottles out there on the market. You can decide if you would like your twins to use plastic bottles, glass bottles, or the bottles with the bag inserts in them. There are also bottles that are great for babies with colic and gas.

Color Coding

If your twins have distinct dietary requirements, it will be important to tell their bottles apart. You can buy pink Avent bottles for one baby and use regular clear bottles for the other.

Different Bottles for Different Twins

There are a few things you can do to keep the different bottles for your different babies straight, particularly if they have different formulas for allergy reasons or nutritional needs. This is especially important in the middle of the night when you're sleep-deprived, or when you have somebody over to help you.

One thing that you can do is to buy different types of bottles. For example, you can buy Evenflo bottles for one baby, and Avent bottles for the other baby. In that case, at a glance, it's easy to tell right away which bottle is for which child.

Make Your Bottles Different

If you have a lot of the same types of bottles, maybe as gifts or from previous children, you can modify those temporarily, or even semi-permanently. There's always a Sharpie or other permanent marker that you can write the initial of the twin around the edge of the bottle. That'll eventually wash off as you're scrubbing your bottles, but it may work for a few rounds, at least.

You can take some masking tape and put it on the outside of the bottle with the name of the child or the type of formula, to help distinguish those, as well.

Keep in mind when you go to wash the bottles or put them through the dishwasher that masking tape can stick to the bottle and leave sticky residue behind. You may want to use masking tape temporarily and take it off before you wash the bottles.

Solid Foods

After your twins reach six months of age, it is time to start thinking about starting them on solid foods. These new foods will supplement their formula or breast milk through at least the end of the first year, when solid foods become the staples for nutrition.

Look for telltale signs that your babies are ready for solid foods. Can they hold their heads up and move them from left to right? Do they push themselves up with straight elbows when lying on their tummies? Do their tongues move forward and backward when you put a spoon up to their lips? Check for these characteristics and talk with your pediatrician about their readiness.

Always start with one food at a time. This way you can clearly see how they respond to the food. Give each new food a few days to see how they react and if they have any allergic reactions.

Generally, by the time your twins are ready for solids, they will be sleeping through the night. Thus, the need for simultaneous feedings becomes less of an issue.

The dynamics of feeding twins solids are what make this process unique with twins.

When it came time to start our girls on solid foods, we started with rice cereal in the beginning. We put them in the booster chairs in the kitchen. One of us, either my wife or I, would sit between them, we'd scoop out little spoons of cereal and feed one twin. Then we'd scoop up another spoon of cereal and feed the other twin. We'd rotate back and forth.

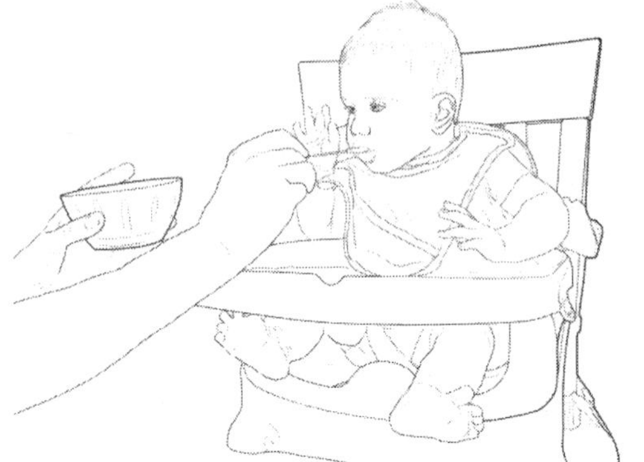

Be prepared to quickly alternate feeding each twin

The funny thing with feeding twins solids is how impatient they can be. Our girls would both want the food at the same time. One sister would see her sibling getting the food and would reach out and try to grab the food herself, or she would start to moan, cry, or try to babble and talk to you and say that she wanted food right away.

It was hilarious to watch them interact with each other and with us when we were trying to feed them solid foods in the beginning. You can never feed them fast enough. You can never feed them enough.

Ultimately this leads to you switching between them as fast as you can and they both end up covered in rice cereal.

If at all possible, try to have both parents feed the twins when it is time for solid foods. This will speed up the process and reduce the twins' frustration.

But this very well may be one of those times with your twins where they will have to take turns. They will be taking turns and have your divided attention for years to come. You don't want your twins to suffer but it is OK to let them take turns.

Make Feeding Time Easier with a Twins Feeding Table

When you have just one pair of hands, many tasks seem impossible. Thankfully, more products are being created especially for twins to help with this. A twins feeding table is just such a product.

If you are bottle-feeding, it is possible to feed both babies at the same time. However, it does require some creativity and patience.

Fortunately, you can now bottle-feed both twin infants at the same time with a twins feeding table for infants. The table is essentially constructed of two infant seats that are molded together. The infants are secured in the baby seats with comfortable harnesses, and the table can be adjusted so that the infants can sit up or lay back slightly. This enables the parent to hold two bottles at the same time, while looking directly at both babies, which is extremely important when it comes to the bonding process.

Table for Two Feeding Table

The Table for Two model is very popular with parents of twins. It will let one person feed the twins at the same time.

When our twins were infants (before Table for Two was created), we'd put two bouncy seats side by side and feed the girls while they were strapped into those chairs. A similar concept is used in the design of the Table for Two. It definitely makes it easier to feed the twins.

Quality tables like the Table for Two have bottle holders and all of the inserts of the seats can be removed and washed. These feeding tables are ideal for newborns, and can be used until the children are about eighteen months old.

If you have space in your home and budget for extra baby gear, a Table for Two would be a good way to go.

Making Baby Food for Twins

Can you make your own baby food for twins?

You may have heard that you can actually make your own baby food at your house; you don't have to buy it in the little jars. Making your own baby food is a very viable option. It is much more cost-effective than store-bought baby food.

My wife and I made our own baby food. Now, when I say "we," I really mean my wife, but the process could not be easier.

Steps to Make Your Own Baby Food

If you have a small food processor or a blender and you've got ice-cube trays, then you pretty much have all the equipment that you need to make your own baby food.

Let's say you're making dinner and you're going go have steaks with baked sweet potatoes and a side of steamed peas. Instead of cooking enough for your wife and yourself, bake a couple of extra sweet potatoes and steam more peas than the two of you would eat.

Once the vegetables are cooked, making your own baby food is a cinch. Put the cooked veggies into the food processor or blender and add a little water. You can put one kind of veggie in the blender at a time or you can mix and match veggies. Push the puree button, and voila! Dinner is ready for both twins and parents.

You will likely have more food than your babies can eat in one sitting, so pour the leftover puree into the ice cube trays and freeze.

Once frozen, pop the cubes of food into a little Ziploc baggie that you can then store in the freezer. You can pull them out whenever you need to give your kids some food. You just warm those cubes of pureed food up and away you go.

Resources on Making Your Own Baby Food

My wife used a great book called "Super Baby Food" by Ruth Yaron. This book has a lot of recipes of baby foods that you can make for your twins, and we used a lot of these great recipes. Our girls were very receptive to homemade baby food.

You'll find additional recipes on websites like wholesomebabyfood.com.

Advantages of Making Your Own Baby Food for Your Twins

One of the great advantages of making your own baby food is that it's going to be cheaper in the long run. Those two extra sweet potatoes you just baked up for dinner probably cost you $1.50 to buy and will feed both babies for three to six meals depending on how much they are eating. A jar of baby food costs about $1.00 in our area and you'll need six to twelve of those to get the same amount of food.

It's also a space saving option if you don't have cupboard space to store 30-40 jars of baby food.

Making your own baby food is a time-saver. In addition to streamlining food preparation like we talked about earlier, you save time in that you don't have to make trips to the store if you run out of baby food. You can just make more.

When you make you own baby food, you'll know where the food came from. You know that if it's fresh produce, it's going to be healthier, fresher, and it's going to taste better. An extra benefit is that you and your wife will likely eat healthier too!

When Not To Make Your Twins' Baby Food

Now, you probably do not want to make your own baby food if you don't like cooking or don't do it regularly. So if you don't want to pick up a new hobby, you may want to cross it off the list, even though it's pretty easy. If you're averse to the kitchen, then you might want to avoid making your own baby food.

Making Your Twins' Baby Food is Easy

Making your own baby food is a viable option for twins. You're making the food in bulk. You'll cook up a whole squash or several sweet potatoes. You'll open a banana and mash it up and feed it to the twins. You slice open an avocado and mash it. Applesauce is an easy option that can be bought in a large jar for multiple meals for much less than a one serving baby food jar. You can make any food you see in the baby food aisle plus so much more. When you make a batch of food for the ice cube trays, that food can then be used over several days or weeks when feeding your twins.

Our girls did great with our homemade baby food, and they really are great eaters, even to this day, several years later. They have still had their picky phases, as all babies do, but they have been willing to try new foods easier and eat a broad array of foods. We really attribute it to them getting great food early on.

How to Clean Up the Kitchen Floor After Twins Eat

Babies are messy eaters.

Twins combine each other's messiness to create a perfect storm of mess that seems to be larger than the sum of each individual baby's mess.

Once your babies are eating solids and feeding themselves, your twins will make a mess with every single meal that they eat.

This means that there will be food not just all over the twins (faces, arms, legs, in the diaper, inside the clothes, etc.), but there will be food on the floor, walls, table, ceiling, and on you.

Cleaning the floor is one of my least favorite tasks and probably isn't your favorite, either.

By the end of the day, you'll find that your twins have covered your kitchen floor with food crumbs, spills, remnants, and rejected nibbles.

You may be tempted to clean these up right away. Granted, if your twins are your first kids, you may think that is the only option.

However, after you have a few kids, you realize that messes are inevitable and you can't immediately clean up every one of them. The messy kitchen floor is no exception.

Clean up wet messes right away, let everything else wait. When you let regular food wait on the floor, it starts to dry out and then becomes that much easier to sweep up.

So waiting to sweep up the kitchen floor actually works to your advantage because all those dried breadcrumbs, cracker pieces, pieces of rice, and hardened noodles sweep up all the easier when they aren't fresh.

Of course if you have a dog, this will be when he really starts to love the babies and you'll get a clean floor to boot.

Twins Swapping Food and Drink

Your twins will trade food and drinks during meals and snack times.

So how do you know how much each child has eaten or had to drink? Once solid food consumption starts, it is less critical to need to monitor exact intake levels.

We sat our twins in booster chairs next to each other when they started eating solid foods.

Due to their proximity to each other, they tended to swap food, sippy cups, spoons, and anything else on their trays.

Your twins may very well do the same.

Our girls would eat what they wanted and leave the rest. If they wanted more food, we taught them to use baby signs to indicate as much. (If, by the way, you want some sanity in communications with your little ones read "Baby Signs: How to Talk with Your Baby Before Your Baby Can Talk" by Linda Acredolo.)

So even if there is food swapping going on, your kids will be able to self-regulate their intake.

However, we found our girls were still swapping sippy cups. This created a problem because we wanted to make sure that they got the amount of milk they needed or the vitamins we snuck into their juice.

Our solution to managing the swapping: different color cups.

It seems simple because it is. Remember, just because your babies are twins doesn't mean they have to have everything identical.

Use color differences to your advantage at mealtimes and you will be able to easily see the food or liquid intake of each of your kiddos.

Twins Have Different Food Preferences and Tastes

Even though we have identical twins, they have very distinct food preferences. Your twins will likely have differences in their tastes as well.

You can't force both twins to be the same. They are individuals and will readily share that uniqueness with you all the time. This means that they won't necessarily eat the same thing at every meal. It is also fun to watch which food each of your twins will reach for and eat first.

Keep offering new foods to your twins. It can take between ten and fifteen attempts of offering a food before a child will consistently eat it. So don't give up too early!

Try variations of the same food (for example: steamed vs. baked vs. grilled) or include the new food mixed with older favorites.

Even from an early age, treat your twins with respect as individuals. Describe what you are doing and what they'll be eating.

We typically offer all the foods that come with the meal and then will ask them if they want more of something. If you rely only on asking them, they will likely stick to their favorite foods and never try anything new.

Each of your twins will watch the other for cues on what is acceptable behavior. When one twin devours a certain food and clearly enjoys it, the other will likely be persuaded to at least try the food.

Likewise, when one twin flatly rejects dinner, the other will likely follow suit without even trying it, unless hunger is persuasive enough.

As our twins reached toddler age and we could reason with them, we'd highlight and praise the positive behaviors we liked to see so that the other twin would desire similar praise.

Don't get too comfortable with one twin eating a certain way because it will likely change sooner rather than later.

Stop Playing, Pay Attention, and Eat Already!

In case you haven't already noticed, kids are easily distracted. They seem to go after whatever suits their fancy in the moment. And that fancy changes with every passing minute.

This becomes a big challenge at mealtime. You'll find that your twins are can be so busy playing that they don't want to eat, even if playing means that they are playing with their food. This is particularly true of toddler twins.

As early as infancy, the challenge may just be getting them to pay attention and eat.

Here are some things to keep in mind to help your kids focus on their food and actually eat.

Eliminate Distractions

Pay attention to what distracts your twins at mealtime. Is it something they can see? Is it something within their reach? Is it something you are doing?

Find and eliminate those distractions.

If the distraction is to run away or wiggle out of the chair, it is totally OK to strap them into their chair. This is easier with a good booster seat or high chair.

Throwing food can also be a big problem. My philosophy is that if they don't have any ammunition, they can't throw anything. This will require that you give them food piece by piece until they can be trusted with a full tray of food. As with any undesirable behavior, even if it is funny, don't laugh. That will only encourage bad behavior.

Inevitably, one of your twins will do something that they shouldn't and the other one will copy it because he or she thinks it is funny. Since twins tend to feed off the energy and mischievousness of each other, you'll see this pattern a lot. We've had success separating the girls to opposite ends of the kitchen table and in extreme cases, facing away from each other. This might require that mom feed one child and dad the other.

If one of your babies starts to slap at the spoon you are using to feed or blows raspberries when food approaches her mouth, it can get really messy really fast. When your child is making feeding difficult, it is OK to take a break and try again in a few moments. If they are eating fine once you get past the crazy hands, you could hold their hands with your left hand while you spoon feed with your right.

Make sure you keep a wary eye on both twins so that a distraction doesn't become a danger. This is particularly true if you have given them a spoon or other instrument to eat with. You don't want your child choking on a spoon because you weren't paying attention.

Make it Fun

Food is awesome. Too often we scarf down our meals and don't actually enjoy them. If you seem stressed and indifferent about the food you are serving, your kids will typically follow your example.

Celebrate how great your food is and make it fun. The older your kids are, the more creative you can get with presentation or names of the meals. In my house for example, instead of Sloppy Joe's we call them Sloppy Daddy's.

Positive Praise

Never underestimate the power of positive praise when your kids are eating properly. As infants this can be a soft touch and gentle voice reassuring them. As toddlers, this can be big smiles, cheers, or high fives.

CHAPTER FIVE

Sleep

Should Twins be on the Same Sleep Schedule?

You could be altruistic about this topic and answer, "I'll do whatever is best for the babies," but by the time you hit your second or third sleep-deprived night, putting your twins on the same sleep schedule is going to sound pretty nice.

In the last chapter, we talked a little about Tracy Hogg's "The Baby Whisperer" EASY steps. If you remember, the baby [E]ats, has some [A]ctivity time, and goes to [S]leep. Then [Y]ou can relax a little.

We've found that getting the babies to sleep at the same time is the biggest factor in keeping them on the same schedule.

Caring for twins overnight in those early months is a handful, to say the least. If you don't have a 1:1 adult to baby ratio with twins at night, you're going to run yourself into the ground very quickly. Stop right now and get help.

My wife and I found it worked best when one daughter woke up hungry, to wake the other daughter and feed her at the same time.

This helped us avoid servicing one baby, getting her back to bed, with us crawling into bed just to be pulled back out to help the other baby. (Or trying to remember whose turn it was to get up with which baby in the middle of sleepy stupor!) The sleeping twin we woke up didn't always eat as much as her sister, but she still typically got enough to hold her over until the next feeding cycle.

If it is just you (or your wife) taking care of the babies during the day, then it might be to your advantage to have the twins on a slightly staggered schedule. This allows the caregiver to be able to feed and diaper one baby at a time. This will mean that there will be a little less time for you, and it may feel like you are on a never-ending cycle of feeding, changing, and napping babies all day long. That's because you are.

If you've got a helper, keep the twins on the same schedule and do everything in tandem. As you grow in your caregiving skills and/or after help goes home, you may find that you're able to keep the twins on pretty much the same schedule. It is possible to feed them at the same time or in rapid succession and get them down for naps at the same time.

The older your twins get, the easier it will be to align their schedules. Just remember–about the time you get comfortable with your routine, something will change. Roll with it.

Children respond very well to routines. This is especially true with twins. Since they are the same age, you can find a comfortable routine that works for both and do that every day. With routines, you twins will know what to expect and will positively respond. There are no surprises for them and it is very comforting and reassuring.

While your twins are still young enough to take naps, you need to make sure they actually get them. You want your twins to nap at the same time so they will be able to go to bed at night at the same time. Both twins won't always sleep when it is naptime, but you need to give them both that opportunity.

Beware the consequences of getting your twins off schedule. They will be sleepy, cranky, fussy, unpredictable and a challenge when they are off schedule.

You'll have life events that mess up the schedule. Vacations, visitors, illness, etc., will all throw a wrench in the works. This is natural and you should be prepared to adjust. Keep in mind that it may take a day or more to get the twins back on track.

> FROM YOUR FELLOW PARENTS OF TWINS…
>
> "You can create a schedule and try to follow it. But most of the time you'll find that the best thing you can do is be creative and enjoy your miracles."
>
> \- *Tamara Curry*

Ideal Sleep Amounts

When your twins get the sleep they need, they will be less irritable and sleep better and longer during the night and naps. We saw that when our kids got the naps they needed during the day, they slept much better at night. Don't keep them up later in the evening hoping that they will be so tired they can't help but sleep. That doesn't work and will backfire.

Your twins' sleep needs will evolve over time. As newborns, your twins will need between 15 and 17 hours of sleep per day. In the first couple of weeks, they tend to fall asleep all the time and there isn't really a discernible schedule. If you adhere to the EASY steps, you will be assured that your babies are getting what they need when they need it, even if there are many EASY cycles during the day. Even though your newborns can and will fall asleep anywhere, it is best to get them in the habit of sleeping in their cribs in a dark and quiet room.

By the one to two-month mark, your twins will be sleeping about 14 hours a day. Most of that will be at night but still in chunks interrupted by feedings. By six weeks you'll start to see some patterns and can hone your twins' sleep schedule.

When trying to keep a schedule, think of it more as guidelines. You're looking for signs that your twins are tired. Stay flexible and adjust nap and bedtimes according to how tired your twins are. If you are too rigid in your scheduling, you'll drive yourself crazy. Each day will be slightly different but the overall rhythm and flow is consistent: wake, eat, play, nap, wake, eat, play, nap, wake, eat, play, bed, repeat.

Around nine to twelve weeks your twins' sleep needs start to shift. They will need to go to bed earlier and their nighttime sleeping should start extending but not necessarily without waking for feedings. Expect about five hours or so of napping during the day.

Once your twins reach three to four months, you'll see real patterns in their sleep, especially during the day. By this time they should have two or three naps during the day. Morning naps typically come within an hour or so of waking up. It may be short but it is important to get the day started on the right foot. The second nap of the day arrives around midday. If your twins take a third nap it likely comes late afternoon, just before dinnertime. Eventually each of these naps will be about an hour to two hours each. We found that if we didn't get the naps going well at the beginning of the day, the rest of the day was much more difficult.

As your twins turn six to nine months they should be getting most of their sleep during the night. Of the fourteen hours or so of sleep they need each day, about three to four come during their two daytime naps. When one twin wakes from a nap and the other continues sleeping, your schedule won't get too out of whack if you let the sibling sleep an extra half hour. However, try your best to keep them synced up on nap schedules. We always put both girls down for naps at the same time.

With their first year approaching, your twins should be down to two solid naps a day and sleeping well through the night.

Between the first and second years, your twins will go down to one nap a day. We found that when we constantly struggled to get a child down for a morning nap it was a sign that they needed to nap once a day. Despite knowing this, this transition always caught us off guard. We'd be frustrated and wonder, "Why isn't she going to sleep?" Once we realized what was happening and moved the child to one nap, things got a lot better. The morning nap is hard for you as the parent to give up since it does offer you a break. Once that nap ends, you'll have more work to do caring for the twins.

How a New Twin Father Can Get More Sleep

I've said this more than once so far, but don't expect to get lots of sleep with newborn twins in your house. You can change your expectations and routine to try and maximize the sleep you can get.

Traditionally, you sleep at night and are awake during the day. Throw all "normal" expectations out the window when caring for newborn twins. There is nothing wrong with going to bed right after dinner at 6:30pm. Any time can be sleep time, so don't say "I can't go to sleep, it's only 7:00." Yes, you can go to sleep whenever you need! The sleep police will not be checking in on you.

Take turns sleeping in shifts with your wife. For example, you can take the midnight to 4am shift of caring for the twins and then sleep soundly from 4am to 8am because you know your wife will take care of any needs during that time. Your twins will have a pattern to their waking and eating. Plan your shifts around those predictable feedings.

Like we talked about in the Food Chapter, during nighttime feedings, both you and your wife can get up to feed the babies. (This works best when bottle feeding.) When you work as a team, you can feed two babies in the time it takes to feed one. Everyone then gets back to sleep faster.

The disadvantage of this method is that no one sleeps for a longer period than the twin babies sleep. You'll get more interruptions during the night.

The best way to get a full night's sleep is to not have to wake up to care for the babies. While that time will eventually come, who will take care of the babies when they wake up until then? I don't recommend pushing all nighttime feeding responsibilities to your wife just so you can sleep unless she tells you that is OK. Or, like we talked about in my first book, you could invite family or friends to come and help with the twins during the night shift periodically, thus freeing you up for a full night's rest.

If you aren't busy caring for the twins during daylight hours, you can take a nap. You have my permission. It can be any time of day (just not while you are driving). After the babies are fed and changed, seriously think about your next activity. Is it more important than some sleep? Choose wisely.

Getting adequate sleep as a parent of newborn twins is a huge challenge. You need sleep to function properly both at home and work. Expect and plan for small stretches of sleep instead of a solid night's worth of rest.

The sleep interruption is only temporary. The good news is that when you awake in the middle of the night, the routine is pretty straightforward: feed babies, burp babies, change babies, go back to bed. You don't have to think too much and that definitely helps in your sleepy stupor.

Crib Sleeping Arrangements

When we brought our girls home from the hospital, we continued the pattern that the nurses established in the hospital: both twins slept together in the same crib.

As newborns all swaddled up for sleep, your babies aren't going to move around much so where you put them is where they will stay. In the crib, this means that you can have both babies sleep together.

Eventually our girls started to wiggle out of their swaddles and move about. We kept our girls in the same crib for several months until they started getting bigger and rotating around. We knew it was time to separate them when were jarred from sleep because one daughter had put her foot on her sister's head and poor sister was crying.

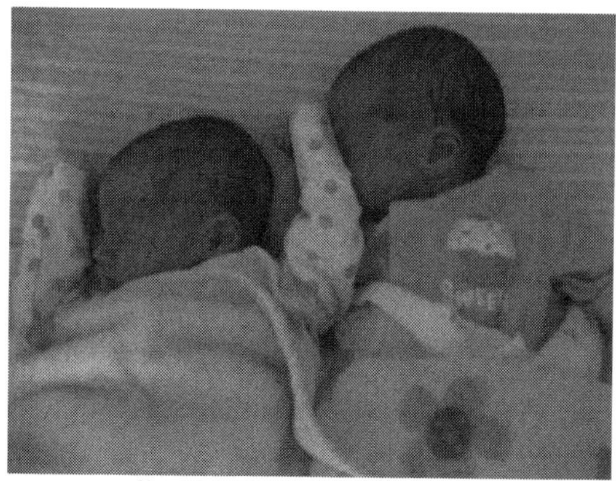

Your twins will cuddle into each other when sharing a crib.

When that time arrived, we put two cribs in the same room, with one baby in each. The girls seemed to miss each other at first but would call out to each other via squawks or gurgles in a form of echolocation (like bats) to make sure their sister was near.

Contrast what worked for us with recent research[1] that has indicated that twins should not share a crib as it increases the risk of Sudden Infant Death Syndrome (SIDS). Our experience occurred before this research was available so I recommend that you consult with your pediatrician when deciding on sleeping arrangements for your twins.

Cosleeping Twins

When we talk about cosleeping, there are really two forms: bed-sharing and room-sharing.

Bed sharing is where you are on the same bed or surface as your babies. Room sharing is where your babies sleep in their own space but in the same room as you.

---

[1] http://pediatrics.aappublications.org/content/early/2011/10/12/peds.2011-2285.full.pdf

The American Academy of Pediatrics discourages you from sharing the same bed as your babies[2]. Your twins are safest with their own separate space. I must have been subconsciously worried about this even though our twins always slept in their own crib. On several occasions when we had infants, I'd wake up in the night in a fright thinking one of our babies was squished between my wife and I. I'd frantically search the bed only to fully wake up and realize that it was just my wife and I.

There are bassinets or cosleepers for babies that can sit right next to your master bed. You might even be able to fit a crib or pack-n-play in your bedroom for the babies. Room sharing has great advantages like proximity and more convenience for reaching over and taking care of the babies in the middle of the night. You can more easily monitor your babies and are quickly alerted to any issues they may have.

One downside of room sharing is that your sleep will be hampered more than just the regular cadence of nighttime feedings. Your babies make all kinds of noises during the night. Most of these can be safely ignored. However, when you are in the same room, you can't help but hear them. You will wake up more than you need.

Ultimately your twins will be in their own room and cribs. Why not start them off there? Both you and they will get in the habit of sleeping in those familiar surroundings.

Just like any number of decisions you have to make as a parent, do your research and see what methods you feel will work best for your family. Move forward with your plan but be flexible in case you need to make some changes.

You'll find a list of cosleepers, bassinets, and pack-n-plays that are ideal for sleeping your twins in your room at www.dadsguidetotwins.com/more.

---

[2] Ibid.

Is it Safe to Have Your Twins' Cribs Touching?

As you browse the Internet or flip through magazines, you'll see lots of images of twins' nurseries that show the twins' cribs touching each other. Is it safe to have your twins' cribs touching? It can be.

In early infancy, when your twins are swaddled and pretty immobile, touching cribs don't present much of a safety hazard.

However, by the time the twins start to move around and/or become attached to a blanket or a stuffed animal of some kind, you run the risk of your twins passing things back and forth to each other through the crib slats. There are risks of limbs getting caught in the slats. One twin could potentially get a blanket over a sleeping sibling's head. At this point, touching cribs may not be the best idea.

Safety-wise, it is recommended that you don't put extra bedding or blankets inside your crib. This will help reduce the risk of SIDS. When your twin's cribs are touching, one twin's blanket may get pushed through to the other twin's crib and cause trouble. You definitely don't want the twins to get entangled or suffocate.

We had our girls' cribs side-by-side, but we did have a walkway between them. This way, my wife or I could stand between the two cribs and reach out and touch both babies. This came in very handy when both of the twins needed some reassurance or some soothing at the same time.

The added benefit was that our girls could also see each other and hear each other more easily, and they did seem to be comforted by that. As our twins got older and were more able to distract each other, we ended up moving the cribs to opposite ends of the bedroom. While they did share the same bedroom, their cribs were far from each other. This helped minimize their interactions with each other when it came time for naps and bedtime, especially as they tended to want to play, talk to each other, and distract each other from the ultimate purpose, which was to go to sleep.

Regardless of the size of room that you have for your twins, especially if they're sharing a room, you should be able to put your cribs close enough for your own purposes, if you need to soothe both twins, but maybe far enough from each other so that they don't reach out and distract each other when they should be sleeping.

Getting Twins Ready for Bed

Bedtime for your twins might just be your favorite time of day. After a long day of work and caring for twins, bedtime offers you the promise of sleeping children and a much-needed break. Establishing a bedtime routine with twins is a great way to control the chaos of your twin life and help your twins at the same time.

Consistency and a familiar routine are essentials for a successful bedtime with your twins. Review your current bedtime routine and see where it differs from what you did yesterday. Think about how you can standardize bedtime so your twins know what to expect every day.

By the time our twin girls were toddlers, our evening routine had expanded to this:

- Baths
- Put on pajamas
- Read stories
- Brush teeth
- Floss teeth
- Have family prayer
- Go potty
- Go to the bedroom
- Say prayers
- Tuck in to bed
- Mom or dad sings them songs
- Good night and shut door

There is comfort in the familiar and repeatable pattern they go through every night. It reduces fighting because they know what to expect. It reduces anxiety. They become comfortable with what is happening because they've done it every night as long as they can remember. Even when one twin is restless, the other will still likely follow the routine and this will help you juggle any bedtime surprises you need to handle as a parent.

We have also found it helpful to have bedtime at a consistent time every night. For us that was between 7:00 and 7:30 until our girls were past the toddler years. This time varied when we had evening activities or plans that took us out of the house. Nevertheless, when we followed the pattern and stuck to a consistent time for bed, the twins (and their siblings) did really well.

Remember to leverage the power of positive peer pressure with your twins. If one twin isn't cooperating, help her twin get ready for bed while giving her positive attention for compliance. The resistant twin will likely follow.

Bedtime with twins can be a challenge, particularly if your twins park their heels like stubborn mules. Not all steps in the getting-ready-for-bed routine are necessary every night. Your twins will be OK if they skip baths for a night or don't floss their teeth for a night. Be patient and offer choices, such as "Do you want to brush your teeth with water or toothpaste?" instead of caving to their "No!" demands.

The beauty of a bedtime routine is that once it is established, almost any adult can run your twins through the steps. This is great for when your kids go visit the grandparents or you want to get out for the evening and hire a babysitter for your twins. The caregiver may change but the routine is the same and this helps the twins adjust to your absence.

Try to establish the routine you'd be happy with for the long term. Once bedtime routines are set, it will be harder (but not impossible) to change later.

The sooner the twins are in bed, the sooner you can rest too!

Transferring Sleeping Twins From Your Arms to Cribs

Occasionally you'll be holding both babies and they will fall asleep in your arms. When this happened to me, I had to decide which baby to put down in the crib first. I'd move one baby to a safe, flat surface, for example, in the middle of our master bed.

I could lean over, with both babies asleep, and gently lay one down on my bed, because it was usually easier to reach down and put her on the bed than it was in her crib (no side rails to block easy access). Then I'd take the sleeping sister to their nursery and lay her down in her crib. I could then go back and get the sister that was still sleeping in our bedroom and move her.

When you're going to lay your babies down one at a time on an elevated surface, please make sure that it is a secure place and your babies will not roll over. Typically, I didn't do this after a girl started rolling, because there's always a danger that they could roll off the bed. But when they're newborns, they're not going anywhere. It should be safe in the middle of your bed for the moments that it takes you to put the other twin in the crib first. But follow your gut and make your own judgments about safety.

If you're in the habit rocking your twins to sleep, you need to stop. While this is an image that storybooks are made of, what the books don't show you is what it feels like when you have a 25-pound (11 kg) toddler who always has to be rocked and soothed to sleep. That is not a habit you want to have.

You want to have your babies be able to fall asleep *on their own* in their cribs without you having to intercede.

When Do Twins Start Sleeping Through the Night?

You won't get to sleep through the night until your twins are sleeping through the night. When do twins start sleeping through the night?

Unfortunately, there isn't a magical date that when reached, all twins decide to start sleeping longer at night. This is a gradual process and every twin is different. You'll even see one twin's sleep patterns differ from the other twin.

Some twins will start sleeping through the night as early as 8-10 weeks. Typically you can start seeing longer sleep stretches around 12 weeks. Many twins wait until 4-6 months.

The bottom line is that every twin is different.

Before you get your hopes up that your twins will sleep long enough for you to get 8 hours of sleep, double check your expectations.

Sleeping through the night for twin infants is a stretch of uninterrupted sleep of 4-6 hours, not necessarily a full 8 hours. However, if you've only been sleeping for 2-hour stretches, 4-6 hours feels really good!

There are several ways you can increase your twins' chances of sleeping through the night.

Do everything you can to get your twins into a predictable and comfortable routine. Every night they should do the same exact things in the same exact order. This helps them know that it is bedtime and that the ultimate step at the end of the routine is to go to sleep.

Your twins wake up in the middle of the night because they are hungry. Try a "dream feed" where you do one last feeding of your twins before you go to bed for the night. Pull the babies out of their cribs and quietly feed them. They will likely stay half asleep but will fill their tummies.

A dream feed then allows the twins to sleep a little longer before needing food. More sleep for them means more sleep for you.

If you'd like more details on how to establish good sleep habits with your twins, I recommend "Healthy Sleep Habits, Happy Twins" by Dr. Marc Weissbluth M.D..

Getting Twins to Sleep Through the Night

Your twins will wake up in the middle of the night for various different reasons.

They may be hungry, fussy, need a diaper change, or just hit the end of a sleep cycle.

Regardless of the reason for waking up, you need to train them to sleep through the night.

Your goal is to get them back to sleep as quickly as possible. The sooner they sleep, the sooner you will sleep.

Think about how you interact with your twins when they wake up in the middle of the night.

Do you turn on the light and greet them with excitement just like it was play time? If this is the case, you are training your babies to want to stay awake.

When you need to care for your twins in the middle of the night, make it as boring as possible. Your twins love to play and interact with you. If you give them the chance, they will want to play even in the middle of the night. Avoid anything “fun” when you are called upon to care for them at night.

Take care of the business at hand quietly. You’ll be amazed how many things you can do for your little one in the middle of the night without saying a word. Additionally, the quieter you are, the less likely you’ll wake up the sleeping twin or your spouse.

Train your twins to understand that light means daytime and dark means sleeping time. With very young babies you can do this merely with actions. For example, don’t turn on the lights in the middle of the night, or use very minimal lighting (just enough to get the job done).

For example, I would turn the closet light on in our girls’ room and crack the door so I could get just enough light to see what needed to be done without waking everyone up.

Once your twins are a little older, you can explain to them that it is still sleeping time when it is dark outside and they need to go back to sleep. However, with a newborn, you’ll need to show through your actions and reactions to their behavior that it is still time to sleep.

If every time they wake up in the middle of the night there is nothing fun to do or see, they will soon skip the boring night and sleep until the exciting daytime has arrived.

Using White Noise to Help Your Twins Sleep

Sometimes, despite your best efforts, getting your twins to sleep is a challenge. You can call in reinforcements. Audio reinforcements. Use white noise to help your babies relax and go to sleep.

When your twins were still in the womb, they were used to hearing a bunch of noise, including mom's heartbeat. You can mimic that noise after birth with a white noise app on your phone, a white noise machine, or even the vacuum cleaner.

A great thing about having a white noise maker is that it frees you from having to feel like you need to be super quiet around the rest of the house. That white noise in the twins' nursery is going to help cover up other noises they're hearing as you talk with family members, do the dishes, or walk around the house.

You can also find apps for helping shush your baby to sleep. This will prevent you from going light-headed when you do the shushing. Shushing mimics the sounds of heartbeats that they were hearing in utero.

When all else seems to be failing, try some white noise and your babies might just fall asleep in no time.

You can find a list of top rated white noise apps at www.dadsguidetotwins.com/more.

How to Get Twins to Go to Sleep on Their Own

The earlier you can get your twins in the sleeping arrangement you want, the better life will be for all. A general rule of thumb is to start as you mean to go on.

Most babies will doze off after feeding while still in the parents' arms. However, when the babies are between six and eight weeks old, you can try putting them down in their crib while they are still awake but already drowsy. Doing this instead of rocking and feeding them until they fully fall asleep can help them learn to sleep on their own faster.

You may find that one of your twins is an awesome sleeper and the other is the complete opposite. If the sleeping child is the "good sleeper," the chances are she will remain asleep regardless of the noise her sister makes. Granted, if the restless twin starts making lots of sharp, harsh noises (i.e., is having a fit), this will probably wake up the other. Remove her as a courtesy to the household sleepers and calm her down in an opposite end of the house. However, don't feel like you have to immediately remove the restless baby at the first sound she makes.

When this happens, do your best to comfort them, soothe them, and be with them. Definitely put them right back in the crib if you have to take them out. This way, they realize that it's time for bed, they need to go to sleep, and you're not going to soothe them to sleep.

For more in depth help with sleep training your kids, check out "The Sleep Lady's Good Night, Sleep Tight" by Kim West. It served us well in getting all of our kids into a good sleep routine.

Can Twins Ignore Each Other's Cries?

We were surprised to find that our girls didn't really wake each other up. It didn't really bother one when the other was crying.

The exception to that was when both of them were ready for feeding time. If one would wake up and start crying, the other would wake up and realize, "Hey, maybe sister's on to something, I think it's time for food too." Then they would both be crying together.

Most of the time they were able to sleep through each other's cries and didn't really seem to affect one another. This was during the newborn phase when both of our girls were sharing a crib. Even after we separated them into different cribs and they were in the same bedroom, they still did not seem to bother each other.

If you are having trouble with your twins waking each other up or disturbing each other with their cries, you may want to consider separating them. This is particularly true if you're trying to get them to sleep and they're crying and keeping the other from falling to sleep. We found that once our girls fell asleep, they were okay, but sometimes they'd keep each other up with their noise. Try putting them in different rooms to get them started sleeping. Later, once they are asleep, transfer them into their crib.

You don't have to rush in right away when one of your twins is crying. Don't be afraid that the other twin is going to wake up immediately and start crying as well. Give it a moment. See what happens. If your twin needs attention, you can go in and soothe that twin, take care of him or her, and then help the other twin if necessary.

The volume and magnitude of both twins crying at the same time can be overwhelming. It's going to get really loud and you're going to think that there's no way that one baby's cries can not affect the other child. Before you jump to conclusions, first observe and see what actually happens with your twins.

When Do You Stop Swaddling Twins?

When our girls were newborns, we would swaddle them up in receiving blankets every night and at nap times to help them go to sleep. Swaddling helps keep the baby cozy and warm and keeps their legs and their arms tight against their body so they can relax.

Even in those early months, the babies will start to flail their arms around. Since they can't quite control their bodies yet, they're not quite sure what's hitting them and it can freak them out. Yes, your babies are thinking, "Hey, who hit me!" and they didn't recognize it as their own arm or hand. Swaddling your twins helps calm them down and get them ready to sleep.

We swaddled our girls for about three to four months. Eventually, they would start to break out of their swaddle almost every night or every time we put them down for sleep. We'd go in to check on them and there'd be an arm hanging out of the swaddle. Eventually, your babies, too, will start to wiggle and move out of their swaddles and that's OK. It's a natural course of them growing up. We continued to swaddle (even though they would break out their arms) until they were too big to fit in receiving blankets.

One thing to keep in mind is that you need to pay attention to when they fall asleep versus staying asleep. If they're OK falling asleep with a swaddle, and don't break out until they're asleep, keep swaddling them before you put them down. If they break out of the swaddle during the night but they stay asleep, that's perfectly fine. You don't need to worry about swaddling them back up, and you can continue to swaddle them when you put them down for bed.

Once the twins break out of swaddles and they start to get too big for swaddling and receiving blankets, a good alternative is the sleep sack, which you can find online or at most baby supply stores. It reminds me of a sleeping bag where the bottom is enclosed but they wear it with armholes like a shirt. They can stay warm while sleeping but can't escape the blanket. If swaddling doesn't work or your twins are busting out of the swaddles early, you may want to consider a sleep sack as an alternative.

You'll find a list of top rated sleep sacks and swaddling gear at www.dadsguidetotwins.com/more.

The Secret of Separating Twins for Nap Time

As twins head toward their one-year mark, you'll notice that nap times are getting more difficult. Your twins may not fall asleep like they used to.

Now they babble and squawk at each other and neither seems to fall asleep quickly or at all.

To help solve this problem, we started separating our girls for naptime.

We didn't have a spare bedroom in which to put a sleeping girl. Therefore one girl stayed in her crib and the other went into a pack-and-play in our master bedroom.

This separation was great. Both girls started falling asleep quicker and took better naps. When one girl woke up, the other could continue sleeping uninterrupted.

At bedtime, the girls still both went down in their cribs in the same room. They would talk and chirp for a while but we didn't see the same problems that we did with naptime. After all, it was easier to fall asleep when it was dark and there weren't as many fun things to do just outside their door like during the day when the sun was out and their brothers were running around.

If you are having trouble at night, consider using this same tactic and separate them for falling asleep. Once your twins are asleep you can transfer one back to their crib in their bedroom. We did this for a season when our girls just weren't falling to sleep very well.

How to Transition Twins to Big Beds

As a parent, you can take great comfort in the fact that once the twins are in their cribs, you get a break. However, you don't sleep in a crib anymore and your twins can't sleep there forever either.

When our girls were about two years old, my wife and I were talking one evening and heard a thump from the girls' room. I went to investigate and found one of our girls standing next to her sister's crib, talking with her. When we had last left the room, both girls were in their respective cribs.

I put the jail breaker back in her crib and said good night. Almost as soon as I closed the door, I heard that same thump sound. I went in again and saw that the offender had a very large I'm-proud-of-myself smile on her face.

I put her back into the crib and told her to stay put.

My wife and I quickly discussed the safety issues and our options. Since both girls were still awake, we went into the room and took the girls' crib mattresses out of their cribs and put them on the floor. We told them they were big girls now and that they got to sleep in big girl beds. (Rookie mistake!)

Well, they didn't buy it. They bounced around, played, and turned their light on and off for about an hour. We realized our mistake and went and put them back in their cribs (after several unsuccessful interventions). We got the escape artist to stay in her crib by tying a large bed sheet over the top of the crib on each of the four corners. It was enough of a deterrent to buy us the time we needed.

The next day we scrambled to get the girls ready for their official big girl beds. We got two box springs down from the attic, bought two new twin mattresses, and took the girls to the store to make a big deal out of buying new sheets and covers for their big girl beds.

The girls were really excited for their new beds and redesigned bedroom. Unfortunately, they were so excited that sleep wasn't a top priority.

We removed anything that could break from the room as a safety measure and even put child-proof knobs on the door handle on the inside of the room and on the handle to the closet so they wouldn't escape or get into more trouble. We hoped that all the fanfare about getting big girl beds would help them settle into the routine.

First Night

We tucked them in after saying prayers and as soon as we said goodnight and closed the door, they turned into Twinadoes.

The girls pulled all of their clothes out of their drawers, played with toys, bounced on the beds, yelled, screamed, and had a merry old time.

We went in occasionally when we heard cries of pain (typically when one had fallen off the bed), and got them tucked back into their beds. Nevertheless, they weren't calming down even after an hour and a half.

So I went into the room and unscrewed the light bulbs from the overhead light and took the nightlight with me.

Without any light to guide their mischievous activities, they finally fell asleep close to 10:00 pm, which was about 2.5 hours later than normal.

Second Night

The next night we kept the night light in the room, and did the go-to-bed routine.

As soon as mom left the room, the twins bounced up and started playing again. With the overhead light bulbs missing, they only had the nightlight to see with. Nevertheless, that was enough to once again empty their dresser drawers and throw all the clothes on the floor.

There was loud playing, talking, screaming, and even banging/kicking on the door and wall. We tried to ignore all the noise but it was so loud that we feared it would wake up their sleeping brothers in the other room. However, we found that if we went into the room it seemed to reset the timer on their play and they would just continue that much longer.

As with the night before, there were some cries of pain and I'd go into soothe and put the girls back in their beds.

They must have been extra tired or perhaps were getting used to the routine because by 8:30 the room was quiet and they must have been on their way to Dreamland.

Third Night

We did the bedtime routine: prayers, tuck in, songs, and left the girls in their room. They played and made noise but overall were quieter than the previous nights. Around 8:15 one girl started crying like something was wrong. I went into the room (which was dark) and fumbled for the night-light. It was missing. The non-crying girl had it in her hands, with the light bulb in one and the fixture in the other. I put it back together and plugged it in. I tucked the girls back in and left.

Ten minutes later, I heard cries again. The room was dark and once again the nightlight thief was clutching her prize. I plugged it in behind the dressers so the girls couldn't reach it, tucked them in and said good night. They fell asleep shortly thereafter.

The girls didn't empty their dresser drawers this evening. Victory!

Fourth Night

The girls skipped their naps on this day so they were treated to an early bedtime. Good news: all was quiet in the house by 7:10 p.m. My wife peeked in on the girls at this time and they were both–amazingly–sleeping on their own beds.

Nights Five and Six

After almost a week of sleep transition for the twins, my wife and I went out on a date two nights in a row (I know: awesome, right?) and the babysitter reported no problems getting the girls down to bed. By the time we got home, they were asleep on their beds.

Essential Tips for Transitioning Your Twins to Big Beds

- Practice tucking your toddler twins into their cribs with regular pillow and blankets like they'll have in regular beds
- Build up the excitement with your twins that they will soon be moving to big beds
- During the day of moving to big beds, talk about it all the time
- Take the twins to the store to buy the mattresses and/or sheets and bed spreads
- Have your twins help take apart and move out their cribs
- Let the twins help you organize their new room with big beds
- Remove any and everything that can break from the twins' room
- Remove light distractions (overhead lights, night-lights, etc.) that are within reach to be turned on and off
- Lower your expectations of a clean and tidy room when the twins wake up in the morning
- Be consistent. Follow the bedtime routine even if the twins immediately pop up out of bed.

- Minimize going into the room after bedtime unless absolutely necessary
- Expect one or both to fall out of bed during the night.
- While there are guardrails you can buy to keep your kids from rolling out of bed, you could save money by just putting the mattress on the floor. When your twins get the hang of their new sleeping space, add the box springs on the floor, just under the mattresses. A week or two later, go ahead and put the bed on a frame. If you buy bunk beds as a space saving measure, consider waiting to use them bunked until after the transition period.
- Try to prevent them from opening the door. Perhaps child-proof handles on the inside, or if their handle has a lock, switch the handle so the lock is on the outside of the room. You could even gate the doorway if your twins aren't likely to jump the gate.
- Give it some time. The transition won't happen overnight (literally). It may take days or even weeks.
- Remember to be patient and consistent and eventually your twins will come around to the new routine.

Whenever you transition from cribs to big beds, it's going to be a bit of a struggle. We had more challenges and struggles than we anticipated getting our girls to settle down when they transitioned to big beds.

It was a surprise to us that it was such a challenge, because their older brothers had each in turn done very well with the transition from crib to bed. In fact, our older boys would just stay in their bed, because they still viewed it as a crib. They didn't even think they could get out of it by themselves!

With twins, this newfound freedom tends to be too much not to enjoy, especially when you have a ready friend and playmate that you can cause mischief with in your bedroom.

Remember to praise the good behavior that you want to see more of — even if it is minor. For example, if your twins stay on their bed, keep their heads on their pillows, or even just close their eyes, reinforce the good and they will yearn for that approval.

If you've got other children in the house, consider getting them down to bed first so that you can free up your time and your attention to be able to deal with your twins. Or if your other children are older, they will be able to self-entertain while you get the twins bedded down for the night.

FROM YOUR FELLOW PARENTS OF TWINS…

"When the twins were in cots (cribs) that was easy. They were confined to quarters. Soon as big beds came along it was freedom for them. So we had to stay in the room until they drifted off to sleep."

- *Ian Barnett*

How Long Can Boy/Girl Twins Share a Room?

Your twins have shared almost everything since they were formed in mom's belly. Naturally, this may lead you to having your twins share a bedroom. Even boy/girl twins can share a room. This arrangement works great for several years but will eventually lead to the question: How long can my boy/girl twins share a room?

If your family is trying to make the most of your limited space, keeping your twins in the same room may be your only choice. In this case, your twins will know why they are sharing a room and clearly see they don't really have other options, although that won't stop them from asking for their own room frequently.

You can always consider shuffling bedrooms around so different kids take turns in different rooms, perhaps making this swap every year or so. This could give variety to your family's quarters but might not always work if you have only a few bedrooms.

A big transition period for your twins will be when they move out of their cribs and into big beds. During this time of upheaval, you may consider moving each twin to his and her own room and take advantage of the big transition time.

One advantage of this is that each twin (assuming both stay in their rooms) won't be distracted by the other and should go to sleep more easily. However, if your twins find comfort in having each other near, separating them at this time might be problematic.

There is not an official age when boy/girl twins should stop sharing a room. The good news is that by the time this question is pressing, your twins will be able to communicate with you. So ask your twins what they think. Talk with them about what they would like to do. If they are happy in the same room, and you as parents don't have any issues with that, then let them share. Eventually, they will have a strong opinion and will want their own rooms.

Sleep

CHAPTER SIX

Healthy Twins

Your twins are different — even if they may be identical. These differences are highlighted by when and how they reach key milestones.

Don't grow concerned if one twin does something (like crawling) and the other isn't ready yet. It doesn't necessarily mean something is wrong. One of the fascinating things about twins is that you have a side-by-side comparison of developmental milestones. Parents of singletons don't have this luxury. Enjoy and appreciate their uniqueness in reaching milestones. You'll notice differences even from the very beginning.

It is funny how others who don't have twins assume that twins are either totally the same or complete opposites. The reality is that they aren't either; they are just unique and different in their own ways.

How to Survive a Well-Baby Checkup with Twins

Your twins' pediatrician will want to see them on a regular schedule over the several months after birth.

These visits usually involve some vaccinations and checkups on the child's physical and mental development.

How do you survive a well-baby checkup with twins? It's simple: have two adults go with the twins. Preferably this would be you and your wife. If you can't go, then an extra pair of hands needs to be ready to fill in.

On one visit to the doctor, I was late getting away from work and when I arrived at the office, my wife was alone in the exam room, holding both of our daughters on her lap, with both of them stripped down to diapers.

If you think a nurse or the doctor will be able to assist you with the twins during the entire well-baby checkup, think again. You'll spend a surprising amount of time alone with the kids while the nurse readies a shot or the doctor writes some notes in the medical record.

By being prepared with one adult per twin, you'll be enabled to:

- not have to worry about the other twin while you wrangle the one in your arms
- soothe and comfort the distraught baby that just got a shot
- get the babies undressed and dressed quickly
- distract a baby as needed while the sibling is evaluated by the doctor
- keep a baby warm (it seems doctor's offices are always cold)

Bottom Line: Don't go alone to a well-baby checkup with twins if you can help it and please, don't make your wife go alone.

Bonus: Many times when I've gone to a well-baby checkup, I've thought of questions to ask the doctor that I hadn't mentioned to my wife beforehand. So if you go, not only do you get your questions answered, but you both get an update on your twins at the same time.

Do Twins Develop Faster than Singletons?

Since your twins are in close proximity all the time, they will watch each other and learn from each other. Will this help them develop faster because they can feed off of each other's progress and development?

Your twins aren't necessarily going to develop faster than a singleton child would. Since each twin is unique, they won't follow the same development course and they will likely pass their milestones at different times.

Your babies are going to go through several different milestones. Physical milestones like teething, rolling over, and sleeping through the night are often based on an individual twin's physical progress and not necessarily the experience of his or her sibling. Children develop at their own pace.

On the other hand, I feel like skill-based milestones like walking, talking, reading, etc. tend to be more influenced by peer pressure and what the sibling may be doing. Your twins can definitely feed off each other's progress in that regard, particularly if you as a parent are positively praising the progress that one of your kids is making. The other twin is going to see that praise and want some of that same attention. That can be used to your great advantage. When one of your twins starts to do something that you like, praise that twin verbally and reinforce the behavior they're doing to encourage the same behavior in the other twin.

Twins are typically born earlier than singleton babies, and as such, they may have a slower development track than a singleton baby. If one of them starts a certain development later than a typical singleton would and if you're waiting for the other twin to follow suit, both of them may be delayed longer than you were expecting. In that case, having twins may not accelerate development because they're both lagging behind what a singleton's schedule may be.

What happens if your twins are developing at different rates or reach milestones at different times? For example, one of our girls crawled before the other. When it came time to walk, the same girl was ahead of her sister. Staggered developmental milestones does have its advantages. It allows you to focus on one at a time as they might need extra help or attention. We'll talk about this more a little later in the chapter.

If you are concerned about the progress of your twins, talk to your pediatrician about their physical and mental development cycles. With well-child checkups, you should get a really good picture from your doctor of the types of things that your children should be doing at that level. Your doctor can tell you what to work on with them to develop their motor skills, speech, and development.

Twins don't always get sick at the same time

When our daughters were infants, one got sick with roseola. This was marked by several days of high fever, a fussy baby, and interrupted sleep for both her and her parents.

During this bout with the illness, her sister was just fine. That, of course, changed about a week later as the previously healthy twin took a turn with the high fever.

Keeping one of your twins indefinitely healthy while the other is sick is a losing battle. Since both will eventually get sick, you might as well prepare for the inevitable.

When one of your twins gets sick, go to the doctor. You'll learn what is wrong, get a treatment, and pay your insurance copay or deductible. When the second twin gets sick, you'll then know what to do and can save the time and money of going to the doctor.

However, only treat the second twin the same as the first if you are sure that she has the same illness. When in doubt, call your pediatrician.

Having one sick baby is a miserable experience for everyone. Odds are you can't really give the baby any medicine other than Tylenol so the baby suffers through the symptoms. You, as a dad, also suffer because of the increased burden of care both day and night that a sick baby requires.

If that is the scenario with one sick baby, the fun doubles when both are sick at the same time (which also happens!). So when only one baby is sick at a time, that is a good thing. The healthy baby can hopefully self-entertain while you provide more care to the sibling.

Washing your hands is important anyway but deserves to be restated here. As the caregiver, you can keep yourself healthy and help control the spread of disease by washing your hands regularly.

With sick baby twins, it may feel like the "wash your hands" principle, while sound, isn't practical. You've got a sick baby (or two) that is sneezing, coughing, drooling, and the like all over herself and you. Is washing your hands really going to help? Yes. Will it help all the time? No, but it is worth the effort.

Watching the progression of illness through your twins is another reminder that even if your twins are identical, they aren't exact copies of each other in life experiences. The twins' environment and their actions now dictate a lot of what happens to them.

How to Keep One Twin Healthy When the Other is Sick

Every time one of our twins gets sick, we have to ask ourselves: does it matter if the other kids get sick too? Is this one of those colds or stomach bugs that they'll get eventually anyway? Does this "build their immunity"?

These are very subjective questions and the answers really depend on your parenting style. Generally speaking in our house, if the child doesn't have a fever, we aren't too concerned if the other kids catch it. That said, when in doubt, always give your pediatrician a call.

Keeping your twins from spreading their germs is an almost impossible task. When your twins are infants, you can't teach them good health habits and they can't take care of themselves.

Toddlers and older kids don't always practice good hygiene, will forget to cover their coughs and sneezes, and tend to do a poor job washing their hands.

If you want to improve your odds of preventing the spread of the illness, you could isolate your sick twin in his or her room. Avoid sharing clothes, toys, towels, kitchen supplies, etc. that the sick twin uses.

Keeping your whole family healthy starts before anyone gets sick. Teach your twins how to effectively wash their hands. We like to have our kids sing "Happy Birthday" twice while scrubbing their hands so they know they washed long enough.

Teach your twins to cough or sneeze into a tissue or into their elbow or sleeve. They should never sneeze or cough into their hands. You can make it a game and your twins will laugh hysterically as you pretend to sneeze into your elbow, but as they see it over and over, they will understand what to do.

While caring for your sick twin(s) make sure that *you* do everything you can to stay healthy. Eat well, get your rest, and wash your hands.

If you get sick on top of having to care for sick kids, things will get really tough. The best sick times in our family are when my wife and I take turns being sick. This way there is always a parent available to carry the load while the other recovers.

Nighttime Care When Both Twins are Sick

When both twins are sick, it feels like you have reverted to newborn twins again. They might need constant care and will likely be up multiple times during the night.

After your twins are old enough and start sleeping through the night, you get spoiled. When an interruption comes along, it will be a switch to handle middle-of-the-night awakenings.

During the initial newborn phase, you got used to the pattern of round-the-clock care and worked out a system between you and your wife to care for the twins during the night. Remember those lessons and put them to use when your twins are sick. Before you go to bed at night, talk with your wife and make a plan for the overnight hours.

Perhaps you will split the night shift with your wife. “Honey, if the girls wake up between now and 2 a.m., I’ll take care of them. You go from 2 a.m. until the morning.”

This sets expectations with your wife and puts a little reminder in your subconscious that will alert you to get out of bed when you hear cries instead of just ignoring them.

Lay out the supplies you’ll need for late night baby care before you go to sleep. Put the thermometer, Tylenol, tissues, water bottle, etc. all where you’ll be able to easily locate them.

Remember, you’ll wake up groggy and won’t be able to think straight. Make it easy for yourself.

Just like you need to keep a log with your newborn twins, you need to do the same when they are sick. This is particularly true if they are running a fever. You’ll need those temperatures to let the doctor know in the morning if things are getting better or worse. Record medicine dosages and time the medicine was given so you don’t overmedicate (or dose the same twin twice if they are both sick).

Put the log and a pen next to your other supplies so that both you and your spouse know what happened while the other was doing the caretaking.

No matter your plan, the time will come when both your little ones wake up crying and sick in the middle of the night. It will be impossible for one parent to care for both. So go get your spouse or let her wake you up. Regardless of whose “shift” it is during the night, there may be a time when all hands are needed on deck.

Don’t worry; your twins won’t have that cold or virus forever. A couple of sleepless nights and things should be back to normal.

Set up your plan, communicate it clearly with your spouse, make your preparations, and you’ll be able to weather double sick twins like a pro.

You can download a sample log for keeping track of your sick twins at www.dadsguidetotwins.com/more.

Two Babies Means Double the Medical Expenses

It may come as no surprise that twins will typically cost you twice as much as a singleton baby.

Even though I know this (boy, do I know this!), I always feel a pinch of pain when I have to take both girls to the doctor and pay two insurance copays.

This may be because I'm used to paying a single copay when I go to the doctor or when I take one of my other children to the pediatrician.

But even with twins, a trip to the doctor appears on the surface to be the same as when you take a singleton. You make one appointment for two babies, particularly for well-baby checkups. You have a single drive to the office. Everyone waits in the same room.

All these events psychologically set your expectations that this is a single visit to the doctor. All, of course, until you have to pay twice.

I have asked (it seems like every time) if I get a two-for-one deal on the copay but the office staff never seems to find that funny.

So if double copays are the reality, you just need to be ready.

Well-baby checkups follow a set pattern (every three months, then every six months, for example), so you can lay these out on the calendar and budget your money accordingly.

Build in a buffer of savings for the inevitable sicknesses that will come.

We've also used a Flex Spending account that my employer offered to help standardize our health expenses and get a tax break in the process.

Remember: two babies equal double copays. Don't be surprised or caught off guard by this, but be ready by budgeting and saving for them.

And if you find a pediatrician who will give you a two-for-one on copays, I want their phone number.

Why Vaccination Day Is the Saddest Day

One of the saddest things you will do as a dad is hold your babies down while they get a shot at the doctor's office.

Hopefully you are helping your wife out and going to the doctor with her and the twins for their well-baby checkups. If so, you will be called upon to do a necessary – albeit truly saddening – task.

Your twin babies will need vaccination shots at nearly every well-baby checkup.

During these visits, the nurse will have you hold your baby down while they poke the needles (often for multiple vaccinations) into your babies' thighs.

If you have any love in your heart for your babies, this job will make you an unhappy daddy.

The simple act of holding your baby down will undoubtedly cause them to cry and start to wiggle. Even if you can keep them happy, the needle poke will turn on the tears.

Your baby will go wide-eyed as she realizes that she just got poked. After a second pause, the cry/scream will emerge from her wide-open mouth and her eyes will start to tear up. She may even stop breathing momentarily.

Yes dad, you get to watch this not-so-joyful sequence of events as the nurse repeatedly pokes your baby's legs. You get to watch not just once, but twice (unless your wife has mercy on you and takes a turn holding down the other twin).

To add to the misery, your baby is looking right at you. Your face. Your eyes. So when your baby feels that intense pain from the shot, she is looking right at you. You'll hope that she doesn't associate the poke, the pain, the suffering with you.

As your twins get older, they will realize what this process is all about and will start to hate the nurse, not you. But in that first year, you need to be ready.

Hold them during their shots because you love them and calm them after the fact so they will know and feel your love for them.

How to Handle Teething Twins

Just when you think you've made it through the newborn craziness and figured out your twins and their routine, a new challenge will appear: teething. Your twins will start to sprout teeth, and the journey won't be so pleasant.

Expect your twins to start teething between 4 and 9 months. This typically happens around 6 to 7 months but can vary from child to child. Even between identical twins, you'll notice that there is no identical teething. You'll see different symptoms, timing, and reactions between your twins.

Your kids' teeth usually start popping out in the middle front and then fill in by age 2.

Since you won't necessarily see the new tooth right away, look for symptoms that could indicate your twin is teething:

- drool, and lots of it
- low grade fever
- chewing and biting everything
- discomfort
- schedule craziness
- crying for no apparent reason

We used Infant Tylenol and Orajel (a topical pain killer) to help the babies feel better. Be sure to consult with your kids' doctor on dosing amounts and frequency.

The twins also found some relief with teething toys, anything cooled in fridge, or a cold wet washcloth to chew on. If you don't give them something to chew on, they will find something. They will chew on their hands, feet, clothes, you, or anything they can grab.

During teething, we had to revisit what we did during the newborn phase: swaying and comforting them in swings or bouncy seats.

Do your best to keep your twins eating and sleeping. If they skip eating, keep trying.

Remember that the crying is not your fault. Don't take it personally. Those teeth will eventually come through and you'll be on to other challenges.

When Do Twins Start Interacting with Each Other?

As infants, we found that our girls would snuggle into each other as they slept in the same crib. That seemed to be kind of reflexive, since they were probably doing this kind of activity while they were still in the womb.

Each set of twins is different, but look for them to start recognizing each other and acknowledging that there is somebody else there between four to six months. Our girls were intentionally interacting with each other by about eight to ten months.

Infants tend to be in their own little worlds interacting with what's directly in front of them. They completely ignore their sibling, even if the sibling is right next to them or touching them. One twin may be more interested in the other before that feeling is reciprocated.

Infants get distracted very easily in early months as their attention span is extremely short. They may notice their twin sibling but not focus on that sibling for much more than a few seconds. At around eight months the competition begins. This is when the twins could be crawling around, and when one twin is not getting something that they want because the other twin is getting it, they're going to start to notice that.

Having your twins interact and play with each other is a two-edged sword. While it is extremely cute and fun to watch, be prepared for the inevitable moment when both twins want the same toy at the same time. This will lead to physical interactions like grabbing, hitting, or biting that you'll want to try and redirect to more positive behavior.

One of the hopes of any twin parent is that their twins will become great friends. Our girls would play and interact with each other, but it wasn't until they could actually talk that they started to play together a lot and be friends. They had their own little gibberish and language that we wouldn't necessarily understand. Once they could start to babble to each other and start to understand each other, and ultimately when they started to speak clearly, that's when they would do more playing together.

Just because your kids are twins doesn't guarantee that they will get along. Honor that when you can, but realize that being a twin may be a crash course in human relations for your twins.

In the very early months, your twins are probably not going to pay attention to each other. Once they get into the toddler ages and beyond, your twins are going to do a lot of playing together. As their needs evolve, they'll realize that the other twin may be getting attention when they want it. But ultimately, they'll start to play together and interact with each other, and then they'll start to get into trouble, and that's part of the fun of having twins.

Twinproofing Your Home

The safety of your twins should be one of your top priorities. As such, twinproofing your home is something you need to do.

Twinproofing is how you childproof your home when you have twins.

Child proofing comes in stages, as your twins grow. When they're newborns and you bring them home they're not going to immediately run over and start putting their fingers in the electrical socket or climbing down the stairs. That's just not going to happen right away. As your twins grow, you're going to start to see more and more risks within their reach. That's good for us as dads because it gives us a little more time to prepare.

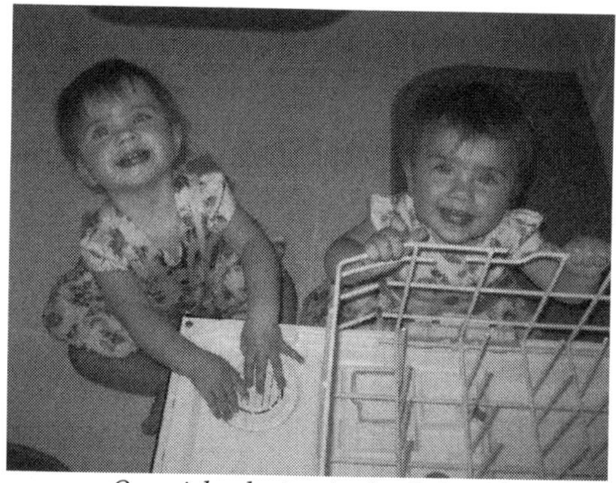

Our girls playing in the dishwasher

As a basic strategy, try to prevent your twins from accessing, reaching, touching, or discovering anything that can do them harm. Let your imagination run wild as you look at your home.

Get down on your hands and knees so you are at your kids' level and look around. Analyze your home and see what trouble you can get into and what things you can reach that you didn't think about as being a hazard before. Even seemingly benign objects could be a problem. Do your best beforehand and get ready to dash to the rescue when something you didn't think could cause a problem is about to.

The kitchen and bathroom are areas where you need to be very cautious because of the overabundance of potential hazards (water, chemicals, sharp objects, etc.).

In the rest of the house, look at power outlets, cords, drawers, shelves, window blinds, lamps, end tables, books, heirlooms, remote controls, plants, and anything else that can be reached by your twins.

While general advice on childproofing your home works for twins, you can't stop there. Twinproofing your home requires extra vigilance and prevention.

Singleton babies can only do so much damage by themselves. Twins, on the other hand, take mischief to a whole new level.

Each of your twins has their own thoughts, imaginations, and crazy ideas of how to get into trouble.

If one of your twins doesn't come up with a creative way to get into trouble, his or her sibling will. Once that idea is formed, it will be immediately shared with the other sibling and you'll have double trouble. Yes, they call it double trouble for a reason.

Two little minds working together to reach the forbidden object on top of the fridge or open the off-limits drawer can quickly invent a method or solution to get what they want.

Your twins will be each other's partners in crime. Twinproofing means you need to account for what your twins can do, not just by themselves, but with each other's help.

Twins will help push each other up to places one can't reach. Twins will combine their strength to break things. Twins will both squeeze into places only meant for one.

One danger zone to consider is the door. Your twins will chase each other around the house and one will turn and slam the door on the other twin. Little fingers or toes can easily be smashed when this happens. Childproof your doors with finger pinch prevention devices you can buy at the home improvement store that keep the door from shutting all the way.

You've got your work cut out for you. Start twinproofing your home today and you'll get a head start on your curious, and often mischievous, twins.

FROM YOUR FELLOW PARENTS OF TWINS…

"I love to watch them around the house navigate every possible open space and crawl space. I have watched them take everything out of the cupboard and climb in and hide. They hide behind chairs, the couch, they love to hide under the covers and make a pretend fort. They love water and love their bath time. I love watching them help each other too. So precious when one is hurt and the other is comforting her."

- Belinda Quesada

Crawling Twins

Having your twins crawl is an exciting milestone for any parent. Once they start crawling there's no stopping them, and there's no turning back. A whole new world has just opened up.

Our twin girls never crawled in the traditional sense before they started walking. They got around by scooting on their bottoms. This was fun to watch, and definitely different from what we saw with their two older brothers, who crawled in normal fashion on their hands and knees before they started walking. Our girls got so good at scooting around on the floor that they could move at quite a fast pace.

Kids typically start crawling between the ages of 6 to 10 months old. However, if your twins were premature or have had any developmental challenges it may take longer for them to start crawling.

Each child will learn to get around in his or her own way, and it may not be a typical crawl like what you're expecting or perhaps what you've seen with other kids. You may see an unorthodox crawl, like an army-man crawl where they're on their bellies, or a crawl like my girls did, where they're not really crawling; they're just scooting around on the floor. Some babies may skip crawling altogether and go straight to standing and then walking.

Scooting around on the floor

If your twins are not moving around at all, I suggest you talk with your pediatrician. If your doctor is not concerned, you might just need to give it a little more time. If both you and your doctor are concerned, perhaps you should consult with an occupational therapist or related specialist, to help get them moving.

Taking Twins to the Dentist

If your kids don't have teeth, they don't need a dentist. Those cute, toothless smiles of your infant twins will eventually give way to a full mouth of teeth. Teeth mean you need a dentist.

Eventually you'll need to take your twins to the dentist. We started when our girls were about two years old.

The challenge of the dentists' office is that your twins will need to sit still while a stranger sticks strange dental instruments in their mouths. While this is true of any child going to the dentist, there are some things to consider when taking both of your twins to the dentist.

If you can find a pediatric dentist, that would be ideal for your kids. Pediatric dentists specialize in caring for kids and know how to help them be comfortable. You'll find a much more friendly environment and staff than at your typical dentist office.

We've found that the pediatric dentists we've used have more open floor plans for cleanings and examinations. My wife's and my dentist, for example, has a more private exam area where you are isolated as a patient. Our kids' dentist has 6-8 exam chairs all in one big room.

With twins you want to find a dentist that will let you have simultaneous cleanings and exams for your children. Talk to the office scheduler to see if this is possible. Ideally, appointments would be at the same time or back to back so that you don't spend your entire day at the dentist's office.

Another thing to keep in mind is how your twins interact with each other and play off of each other's energy, anxiety, and fears. If you can get them both in the same exam room this will let one watch the other.

We've found that our twins tend to look to each other for the behavior they should be exhibiting. So in the case of the dentist's office, if one twin is doing well and sitting still for the exam, the other will likely follow. Having both twins there also gives you the opportunity to use positive peer pressure to your advantage.

Don't show up the morning of the appointment without having prepared your twins for the dentist. Talk about what will happen and what they can expect when they go to the office. There are plenty of children's books you could check out of your local library that illustrate a positive experience at the dentist's office.

As with all things for twins, you'll need to think about logistics and schedules. Try to make an appointment at a time of day they are generally at their best. It might not go smoothly if you introduce them to the dentist during nap time.

After they get used to things, they'll know what to expect and you'll be fine for subsequent dentist appointments.

When One Twin Is Injured

Twins like to get in trouble. There seems to be an escalating spiral of mischief where they feed off the energy of each other until things culminate in an accident or injury.

One afternoon, our girls were playing in the backyard with their brothers. The entertainment of choice in this case was to spin the back tire of their bicycle while poking a stick in the spokes. This made a very fun noise and stimulated the senses of our children.

Unfortunately, little children also have fingers that somehow get put in places they shouldn't go. In this case, our youngest daughter inserted her finger into the spinning wheel. The finger then got sliced open. Ouch!

Mom immediately applied some first aid to treat the finger. Unfortunately, we could only control the bleeding if we kept pressure on the wound. This situation meant that she needed stitches.

We dropped off our older boys at their baseball practice and took our girls to the urgent care center near our home.

There are inherent challenges of taking an injured twin and a healthy sibling to the emergency room.

Most of your attention, rightly so, is on the injured child. If you must bring the sibling along, make sure that you have something for him or her to do.

The non-injured sister was sympathetic to her sister's plight and offered to comfort her and talk to her. However, when it came time for the stitches, we had to keep the healthy sister at a safe distance and entertained. She sat outside the exam room blissfully playing on the iPad while her sister wailed inside the room.

It took both my wife and I to restrain our injured daughter during the quick procedure to stitch up her finger. Not all medical facilities will let two parents into the exam room. But this definitely helped us care for our daughter.

After the procedure, my injured daughter got a freezer pop and was happy as can be. The staff was very sensitive and offered our non-injured daughter a freezer pop as well. When children are young, freezer pops *can* make everything better!

Why You Want Twins to Start Walking at Different Times

As your twins approach the one-year mark, they will start walking. Or at least, try to walk.

You don't want both of your twins to start walking at the same time. Why? Simple: attention, time, and back pain.

When your little ones start moving towards walking, odds are they will start pulling themselves up on the couch, bookcases, or anything else they can reach.

The next phase is where you hold their hands while they take tentative steps around the house.

Gradually, your babies will be so confident in walking (but not independent yet) that they will want you to hold their hands and help them walk (run) around the house. They will want to walk all the time.

You are just one person. It is physically impossible to help two babies walk at the same time, particularly when they are just getting started. A new toddler is extremely unstable and you need both of your hands to help with balance and prevent a disastrous fall or collision.

If both of your twins want to start walking at the same time, you'll have to take turns. Either each toddler takes a turn or you and your wife each take a toddler.

If there is one caregiver–say it is just you or your wife–this creates three problems:

First, each baby will have to take a turn walking and odds are this will produce screams, tears, and maybe a temper tantrum. (Sharing and turn taking is something they will learn sooner than most singletons, but they don't get it at this age yet.)

Second, you'll never get a break.

Third, since you are hunched over all the time to help your little ones toddle about, you'll quickly have some back pain issues.

So, bottom line? Pray that your twins are on a slightly different developmental scale when it comes to walking. It will make life easier for everyone.

CHAPTER SEVEN

Identity

How to Tell Twins Apart

When your twins are born, they often look very similar. This is a big question parents of twins ask: How do you tell newborn twins apart?

Your twins will give you natural indications of which one is which. Additionally, you can help identify them with tricks you can employ.

Obviously if you've got boy/girl fraternal twins, you will never confuse which baby is which. However, when your newborns are swaddled up in their blankets and all you see is their little faces, don't be surprised if they look very similar. Fortunately, if you do mix them up, you can always verify who is who with the next diaper change.

Even identical twins will be born with different lengths and weights. One of your twins may have a more round face or chubbier legs than the other. This may help you tell them apart right away. However, your twins will have weight gains and losses as they adjust to the real world and learning to feed. So don't count on the weight difference always being there.

Your twins' hair may be different colors or lengths when they are born. Your twins may not have any hair at all! Hair may be a good differentiator in the beginning, but since hair does grow, it isn't reliable long-term until you can actually cut and style it differently on each twin. Once our girls' hair grew out, we had one with a very short haircut and the other one had longer hair to help us, friends, and family easily distinguish which daughter was which.

When our girls were born, one had very red skin like she was blushing or hot. Our other daughter was more pale and white colored. Your twins may have different shades of color as well. In our case, the color difference was temporary. So while it was helpful in the hospital, things soon normalized and color wasn't that different.

Look for birthmarks or other natural marks on your twins when they are born. One of our girls had a small red patch on her eyelid. I used that mark to help tell them apart for several weeks before it eventually faded.

Sometimes your babies will be born with scratch marks where their sharp little fingernails left a mark on themselves or each other while in the womb.

You'll notice behavior, personality, and mannerism differences in your twins. Don't rely on these as 100 percent of twins will switch personalities right before your eyes.

As you can see in the physical ways to tell your twins apart listed above, they all seem to change over time (except gender, of course).

Use what you can to tell your twins apart, but be prepared to supplement any physical differences with some systems or tricks that you put into place.

Dressing your twins in different clothes is my favorite method for telling newborn twins apart. We used different colors with our girls. One of them was always in warm colors like reds, pinks, and yellows. The other was always in cooler colors like blues, greens, and purples. This color pattern made it easy to tell them apart across the room and was easy for others to remember as well.

Many parents of twins will paint a toenail on one of the babies to help tell them apart. This works great during the summertime when little feet may be exposed. However, when babies are swaddled in blankets or bundled up for winter, this method doesn't allow instant identification.

As soon as your twins are born, they get medical wristbands in the hospital. These don't come off until you get home and take them off yourself. I even left our girls' wristbands on for a day or two after we got home just to be sure I could rely on other methods to tell them apart.

However you decide to tell your newborn twins apart, you need to be consistent. Help others tell your twins apart by explaining the pattern to them.

Having newborn twins in the house will mean you are fatigued, and there may be some momentary confusion. Don't feel guilty about this as even children born years apart are sometimes called by a sibling's name. Many an adult has recalled being a child of a large family and having their mother or father call them every single one of their siblings' names until they hit upon theirs.

Many parents of identical twins notice distinct differences in their children's personalities within hours or a few days of birth. One may sleep peacefully for long periods of time, while the other may awaken every hour. One child may cry more often than another and want to be held constantly, while the other may be quieter and seem more contented on its own. They have very distinct and unique personalities. They'll have different likes and dislikes and even different propensities to cry or to be fussy or to laugh at your jokes, whatever the case may be.

With time, you can start to see the types of expressions that your twins make in their face or with their bodies that are unique.

When your twins start to talk, their voices and the way they verbalize the words will be different. You'll start to see that distinguishing factor even between identical twins who have identical vocal chords because you'll also notice how they speak differently. They'll use different words or different pronunciations and you'll start to pick up on the quirks and the differences between them.

FROM YOUR FELLOW PARENTS OF TWINS…

"My wife and I were worried that we wouldn't be able to tell Theo and Patrick apart. Would Theo and Patrick look exactly the same?

"We were starting to come to the realization that by naming them during early stages in pregnancy, upon birth and later in life we would not know who was actually who. Our tentative game plan was to sit them down when they were 18 years old - old enough to handle shocking, potentially life-altering news - and tell them, 'We don't actually know who is who. You may be you, but you may also be your brother. We're sorry for the mix-up.'

"With their birth, the potential disaster was averted. Theo and Patrick could not look any more different. Theo, Baby A, never cooperated with the 3D imaging and looks nothing like Patrick (nor their older sister). We're talking Arnold Schwarzenegger and Danny DeVito-esque twins. That parent-to-twin talk we had contemplated in 18 years will not be necessary (some unexpected free-time in 2033)."

- Joe Kenney

Help Others Identify Your Twins

As a parent of twins, telling your twins apart will come naturally. It might not happen right at the beginning, but it will happen.

However, this inherent skill as a twin parent only applies to your kids. When I see other identical twins, at church, for example, I can't tell them apart. I have to rely on context clues like hair style or clothing colors, or be clueless.

Why is this? Time.

Having twins doesn't give you super powers that let you identify any random identical twin.

Having twins gives you time with your twins. Constant contact and interaction helps you differentiate your twins.

Others will be baffled at how you can tell your babies or even your identical toddlers apart. They need help identifying each of your twins.

Associating a name with each twin is key for other people to interact with your children. Your twins will interact with others in the neighborhood, at church, in school, in playgroups, at birthday parties, and more. You won't always be there to help them out, either. (No, you can't make them wear nametags all the time.)

Until your twins are old enough to answer the question "What is your name?" you need to put a system in place to answer it for them. You need to help others identify your twins. Give them something easy to remember that will help them remember which twin is which.

If you've got a boy/girl set, please pick good names for your twins that make it easy to differentiate which name goes with which gender.

For identical twins, you may want to leverage the same tricks that you use to differentiate the twins. This could include different hairstyles, clothing, or even accessories like bows, shoes, etc. Just make sure to communicate what that difference is before dropping off your twins with others.

One trick that has been effective for us is to style the hair differently on our girls. When they were younger, one had bangs and the other didn't. Whenever we explained to people how to tell them apart, they easily remembered because one had bangs. Since this is a semi-permanent trick, people have been able to remember it over time and could easily tell our girls apart.

Notice the different hairstyles

If you can combine a physical difference with some alliteration in the child's name, it will be even easier for someone to remember. For example, "Christie: Curls" both start with the letter "C" and creates a memorable phrase. Or in another family we know, Ryan always wore red and Brandon always wore blue.

Share the secret with those folks that interact with your twins. They will thank you for it by confidently calling your twins the right name without second guessing themselves.

Color-Coded Clothing Won't Work Forever

If you use color-coded clothing to tell your twins apart, keep in mind that this won't last forever.

We dressed our girls differently after they were born. This helped us tell them apart at a glance and helped others tell our twins apart, as well.

However, our little twin babies started to grow up and have an opinion about what they wanted to wear.

What did they want to wear? Each other's clothes, of course.

When your twins are small infants, you can dress them in whatever you want. However, as they get bigger, you'll find that they will start to resist your choice in outfits.

This happened to us at about a year old. By that time, all of our friends and extended family were used to the colors of clothing used to distinguish our twin girls.

Habits with a long history like that are hard to break.

I could no longer walk into a room, see a girl dressed in pink, for example, and assume it was the right daughter. I constantly called out the wrong name to the wrong girl.

Take heart, because by the time your twins have an opinion, there will be plenty of other things to help you tell them apart.

Personalities will be totally different. Your twins' voices and speech will be different. Physical looks (even on identical twins) will be different – especially to the trained eye of a twin parent.

Twins Are the Same, and Yet so Different

Your twins go through the same pregnancy and virtually the same environment from the moment they are born. Yet whether your twins are identical or fraternal, you're going to observe amazing differences. Your twins can be so different and yet so similar at the same time.

Just because twins are born at almost the same time doesn't make them the same person. You're going to observe different behaviors and different personalities in each of them.

It'll give you unique experiences and interactions with each of them so you have certain memories of one twin and other memories with another twin.

You will also have distinct parenting challenges for each twin. You'll be able to master your parenting skills on each of your twins because odds are, they'll have different challenges and behaviors that you'll need to discipline or correct. Having twins that are very different also gives you a lot of variety, which makes for interesting experiences and happy moments in your home.

Take notice of the things that are different and unique about your twins. Enjoy those differences and celebrate them.

FROM YOUR FELLOW PARENTS OF TWINS…

"We have always been surprised by how different the twins are, from the moment they were born (actually my wife says they were completely different in the womb). Despite the fact that they have experienced identical life experiences, they are on different development timelines, and their different personalities demand that we parent them differently (one is independent, the other needs more nourishing)."

- Eric Meyler

FROM YOUR FELLOW PARENTS OF TWINS…

"I think one of the biggest surprises I encountered as the father of twins is how different their personalities really are. I guess I knew this in the back of my head, but never having children before they joined our happy clan, I kind of expected them to be alike because they are twins. It took me a little bit to remember that they are fraternal twins so they are basically two little boys who happen to have the same birthday. They are also going to both learn and develop at their own pace. With our sons, one is the talker. He'll repeat everything you say, especially if you don't want him to. The other is definitely the thinker of the two. He's very methodical in the way he does things, and is a whiz at puzzles. I have learned that it's important to remember to treat them differently. I work with each differently with their strengths and weaknesses in mind. While I'll review colors and shapes with one, I'll throw the ball, and work on words with the other."

- Kevin Zelenka

FROM YOUR FELLOW PARENTS OF TWINS…

"Not only do we have fraternal twins, but they both look and act completely differently, and it made a statement to all of us in the family that they are two individual brothers. In fact, they look like twins of my wife and I more than each other (Anthony looks like me, Brandon looks like my wife Kimberly). They each reached different milestones at different times — Brandon sat up, was first to eat, babbles a lot, and has a lot of hair on his head. Anthony grew teeth first, prefers to be on his belly, crawls, and has very little hair. Both have taken distinct personalities. Anthony loves to crawl, play, and is very wild and active. Brandon is relaxed, prefers sitting up, looking at his books, and just observing the environment. We rarely refer to them as the twins, and were surprised to find out that growing in the womb next to each other and being born the same day is really all they have in common! They are each their own their special little guy!"

- Brian Zufolo

Twins Have Their Own Language

As soon as your twins can make a sound, they will start to "talk" to each other.

Since our twins were in separate cribs but slept in the same room, they could hear each other squawk and make other baby sounds. One girl would squawk and the other would answer with her own squawk. It was like two birds in two different trees calling to each other.

This pattern of twin-to-twin communication continued through their toddler years.

I would frequently catch the girls chatting to each other with some recognizable words mingled with gibberish. Each will respond to the other in turn and thus they carried on a conversation whose meaning was unknown to any observer.

Look for how your twins are communicating with each other. You'll find patterns and behaviors that highlight this phenomena.

What secret codes or sounds are they making that you can't quite decipher but that they seem to understand just fine?

Twins Switch Personalities

Since we have identical girls, we often relied on their mannerisms and personalities to tell them apart.

Be careful if you rely on this too. Twins switch personality traits at will.

For example, one of our girls will be shy one week while the other is a social butterfly. Just when you think that is the pattern, they switch and the social standout now cries hysterically with strangers.

We've seen switching of twin personalities and traits even at an early age in all these cases:

- who is a good eater
- who is a wiggle worm
- who wakes up first
- who takes good naps
- who drinks her bottle in one sitting
- who smiles at strangers
- who makes what sounds (when the girls weren't talking yet)
- who steals toys from the other

It is fascinating to watch the switcheroo happen. Just keep your eyes open and enjoy the journey.

FROM YOUR FELLOW PARENTS OF TWINS…

"The biggest surprise is how different their personalities are and how everyday they change. One day the restless one is OK and the calm one is restless. They never stop surprising you. We have to change our parenting every day."

- *Carolina Comte*

Twins Don't Initially Think of Themselves as Twins

Your twins will recognize themselves as siblings–brothers or sisters–before they realize they are twins.

The label of "twins" seems to be pressed upon your twins instead of being something that they naturally recognize and claim for themselves.

The "twin" label seems to be a reference point that is picked up later in life by the twin herself. Yet from birth, everyone else knows your twins as exactly that.

You may call your twins "twins." Their brothers may call them "sisters" or "twins." Everyone in public will say, "Hey, look! Twins!"

Our twin daughters knew and could verbalize that they were sisters way before they grasped the meaning of the word "twin." Perhaps this is because we didn't call them "twins" when talking about them or to them. We'd tend to refer to them in the third person as "the girls" or "your sisters."

To one of your twins, the other twin has always been there. She is a sister, friend, roommate, playmate, and someone that shares everything.

It is easier to explain to one of your twin daughters that she has a sister and is a sister than explain how babies typically only come one at a time and how she is different.

As your twins grow, see if they recognize that they are siblings before they understand what a twin is.

How to Tell Identical Twins Apart on a Phone Call

It took a while before I could actually tell my toddler twins apart when I talked to them on the phone. The key to hearing the difference is in paying attention before the phone call even happens.

When you are with your twins in person, pay attention to the nuances in speech. You'll notice that they use different words, vocal mannerisms, intonations, and exclamations.

These are the keys to knowing the twin on the other end of the phone call. It isn't the sound of the voice but rather what is being said and how it is said.

Pay attention to how your twins sound. Can you tell who is squawking from the other room in the middle of the night? Can you tell who is calling for you from the far end of the house?

Practice listening and noting the differences between your twins and you'll be able to identify them like a personal caller ID the next time you talk on the phone.

Call Your Twins Individually and Not as a Pair

Once your twins are old enough to crawl, they will find ways to move away from you when you want them to go somewhere or do something.

When you want your twins to pay attention to you, it will be quicker to say, "Come on, girls," or "Let's go, boys," than it is to say each individual name. However, you won't get the response you want by calling them as a pair.

You need to call them individually. You need to call them by name.

Instead of saying, "Let's go, boys," try "Let's go, Michael. Let's go, Bryan."

I've found that calling to the pair as one unit just doesn't work.

Perhaps there is too much ambiguity in the summons. Maybe my girls know I'm talking to them but ignore it because I didn't call them out specifically.

Whatever the reason, my twins respond better when called specifically by name. Try calling your twins individually, by name, and see if you get better responses.

Always Referring to Twins in the Same Order

When you talk about your twins in the third person, you may find that you always refer to them in a particular order.

For example, if you have twin girls whose names are Mary and Beth, you may always talk about them as "Mary and Beth" and not "Beth and Mary".

The pattern that you fall into will be natural and you may not even notice it at first.

The pattern may be the birth order of your twins or even based how the names sound together.

You'll notice the pattern when you start to hear others refer to your twins with the opposite pattern.

Something will sound odd when you hear their names paired that way and then you'll realize what it is: they didn't use the same pattern you do.

Stop and pay attention to how you refer to your twins. What's your pattern?

Help People Recognize Your Twins as Individuals

A common concern of parents of twins is "How can I help people recognize my kids as individuals and not just as 'the twins'?"

It is easy for most people to see a pair of twins and automatically group them together. It is a shortcut because most people don't care or have the time to think about the differences between your twins.

This can be frustrating for you, the parent of twins. After all, each of your kids is unique.

Here are some ways you can help others recognize your twins as individuals and not as a single entity known as "the twins."

Start by evaluating the way you refer to your twins. Others are watching your actions and how you talk about your kids. They will follow your lead.

Do you group the twins together when discussing them? Do you call them "the twins" or "the girls" or use their names like "Bobby and Susan?"

Don't be surprised when others do the same.

Mention your twins individually and by name in conversations with others. If you must group your kids together when discussing something, then refer to your twins as "the kids" or lump all your kids together as "the kids" (if you have more than just the two) so that the twins aren't singled out.

Your example will go a long way toward how those in your household refer to your twins. If mom and dad are always calling the twins by name, other siblings and family members will do likewise.

When you have visitors over at your house, they will never hear about "the twins" – only about each individual by name.

It helps others when your twins look physically different. This is definitely easier when you have girl/boy twins, and can even be easier if there are distinct characteristics of each of your same sex fraternal twins. When people see different-looking kids, they are less likely to group the twins into an automatic pair and will be more likely to treat them as individuals. When you dress your kids identically, don't be surprised when others can't get past the sameness of the pair.

How others refer to your twins can be a pet peeve that annoys you to no end, or it can have no effect on you. You decide how others' comments impact your mood. Most comments about "the twins" are not made with malicious intent. Receive them as they were meant to be received – take no offense and roll with it.

As your twins mature, they will develop very distinct personalities and tastes. These will manifest themselves in appearance and behaviors that will reinforce the reality that your twins are individuals.

Eventually, your twins will have an opinion on the matter and will be able to challenge others' comments themselves.

How to Encourage Individuality in Your Twins

Encouraging individuality in your twins starts with how you treat them.

When an activity is truly optional, avoid forcing one twin to do what the other is doing. Granted, you'll need to make a judgment call here as a parent. For example, if one child doesn't want to color, don't stress out about it. But if one doesn't want to brush their teeth, you might have some stronger feelings about that.

Ask each child what she would like to eat, do, see, play with, or experience. Look for opportunities to do those different activities.

Give each twin the opportunity to help make meals, pick the particular food for lunch, or choose which restaurant you'll be visiting.

Let your twins experience different activities as they grow to see which one they like most. For example, you may find one of your twins gravitates to dancing while the other prefers swimming.

Tell your immediate and extended family that you want to encourage individuality in your twins. Share some of these tips with them and practice them in front of your family members.

Birthdays and holidays are great opportunities to have family members highlight the individuality of your twins. Have two different birthday cakes. Get each twin a different present.

When they are old enough to express their opinion, let your twins pick out the clothes they want to wear. You'll start to see preferences in their respective styles and dress.

Style your kids' hair differently. Like clothing, they will start to have a preference as to what type of hairstyle they have. This will come up with haircuts and also on a daily basis (for example, pony tail or pig tails? Spiked hair or combed down?).

Avoid always dressing your twins in identical outfits (especially as they get older). These matching outfits are cute every now and then but they fail to reinforce that your twins are individuals.

Celebrate these differences and encourage each twin's development of unique hobbies and personalities.

Ways Your Twins Show Their Independence

Your twins will have a lot in common, even if they aren't identical. Nevertheless, they will start from an early age to show you how independent they can be in their behaviors and actions. Here's what to look for as your twins start to exercise their independence.

When your twins are infants, their opinions are expressed with tears or physical outbursts. When they are toddlers, these opinions may turn into temper tantrums. As your twins develop their speaking skills, they will start to argue with you and express themselves with what seems like the astute logic of a trial lawyer.

Your twins won't always want to do what you'd like them to do nor continue to do what they've always done. One twin won't always want to do what the other twin wants to do. Each of your twins is unique and will show you as much through their daily actions.

Your twins will not always want to eat the same thing they've always eaten. An interesting trait-switching pattern we've seen with our twins is that one has been a great eater and the other a little pickier. In addition, when one twin eats really well, she loves the praise we give her. The other twin will then, in turn, want the same positive reinforcement.

Study the behaviors and preferences of your twins at mealtime. How do they exert their independence with food choices or in behaviors relative to each other?

Look at your twins' preferences with clothes. Are they similar or different from each other? How are they expressing their independence through what they want to wear (even before they are teenagers)?

Should you put your twins in a dance class? Soccer? At first you might get away with both going to the same activity. However, their opinion will eventually rule the day and you just might end up with one twin in karate with the other in gymnastics. One twin will like to draw while the other will like to dress up.

A variety of "likes" and "dislikes" is what makes your twins so fun. You never quite know what to expect.

How to Give Enough Individual Attention to Twins

Your attention will be divided with twins. Particularly in the early months, your head will be spinning as you try to take care of your twins and family. With all the chaos, how can you be sure to give enough individual attention to your twins?

When caring for twins, it is easy to jump in and mindlessly care for whichever baby is in front of you. While this will work in meeting the immediate need, you're missing out on an opportunity to build a relationship with each of your twins.

One way to guarantee you give individual attention to each of your twins is to take turns with the child care tasks.

Look at the tasks that will happen multiple times a day or week (especially when the kids are young). How you can take turns caring for each child in these instances?

Take turns bottle feeding each twin or burping them after they've been fed. When they are older, you can spoon-feed one or sit next to a different toddler at every meal.

Talk to your child when you are changing diapers. Yes, you can go beyond commenting on the stink and mess. You will learn quickly how to tell an impromptu story in an animated voice to distract a squirming child!

Take turns dressing your twins. As they get older, talk with each as you help him or her get dressed and find out their preferences and styles.

Bath time in our home has been traditionally a dad duty. While the efficient engineer in me wanted to throw all the kids in the tub at once, I enjoyed the single baths I'd give my infant children since I could focus all my attention on one at a time.

Story time is a favorite in our home. Sit each twin on your lap in turn and read each a favorite book or story.

In the spirit of efficiency, it is too easy to give a group good night and song and then leave the kids' room and move on to your kid-free evening. However, to help spend individual time with each twin, hover near each twin's crib or sit on the edge of her bed to sing a song just to that child.

While your twins will likely play with each other most of the time, there will be moments when you'll find one twin playing or reading by herself. Take that time to sit down with the child and talk about what she is doing. Yes, you can even play one-on-one!

When you make a focused effort to bond with your twins, you'll see opportunities to give individualized attention to each.

FROM YOUR FELLOW PARENTS OF TWINS...

"Our twins are only four months old and already have surprised us many times. I still cannot get over the fact that no matter where in the house one of the twins are, as soon as you put one down the other one will wake up the second you do, knowing your arms are free, just for them."

- Brock Easterling

How to Bond with Your Twins

As a father of twins, you want to bond with your twins and build a strong, lasting relationship.

The key to this bond with your twins piggybacks on the principle we just discussed, that of spending one-on-one time with each of them individually. The more time you spend individually with each child, the deeper and stronger the bond you develop.

The best time to bond with infant twins is when you are helping with their daily necessities. When our twin girls were still infants, I loved to take turns feeding each one. As they slowly drank their bottles, I could study their faces and expressions and talk with them about the great future that was ahead of them.

My favorite bonding activity with toddler twins is to take them out to lunch one at a time. You can have father/son or daddy/daughter lunches with each of your kids too. I've found that getting out of the house with one of the twins helps focus all my attention on that one child. It is a great way to build and strengthen my relationship with each child.

If lunch doesn't work for you, consider other outings with just you and one of your kids. This could be a Saturday activity, an errand to the store, or another time together that best meets your schedule.

Make these one-on-one times a routine event and your kids will look forward to this tradition with dad.

Regardless of the age of your twins, you can make time for each individual child. This time focused on each child will be the foundation of a strong bond and lasting relationship with each of your twins.

FROM YOUR FELLOW PARENTS OF TWINS…

"At almost 11 months old, everything is funny around them. They can laugh their hearts out at anything, and that's probably the funniest thing. I try to make them laugh with weird voices and faces, and when they start laughing hysterically, I end up laughing with them!"

- Santiago Lopez

Which Twin is Older?

Should you tell your twins which one of them is actually the oldest?

Your twins aren't going to ask you this question when they're infants. Even though twins are born on the same day, one of them came out of mom before the other. Most likely it's at least a couple of minutes apart, depending on the type of delivery.

This question often comes up from other people before your twins will bring it up. Strangers or family or friends will ask, "Which one is older?" In that case, you don't have to answer if you don't want to. You can simply say, "Hey, they're twins. They're the same age. They were born on the same day."

When it comes time to tell your twins, consider a few of these things. First of all, it might not even matter to them which twin is older. If they don't bring it up, maybe you don't have to bring it up either. Alternatively, you can bring it up preemptively so that they know, "Well, you were born two minutes before your sister."

In our situation, we've got identical twin girls, and one of our girls was born about two minutes before her sister. We haven't really made a big deal about this fact. They both know who's the older one and who's the younger one. It doesn't seem to matter, because as a family we take turns rotating through activities or taking turns for whatever we are doing. If it's taking turns doing an activity with daddy or if it's taking turns saying a family prayer, we rotate all these through all of our kids, and so there's really not discrimination against the older or the younger child in the mix.

If you as the parent don't make a big deal about which twin is older and you don't give preferential treatment to one over the other, odds are your kids will follow your example. So if the older kid doesn't get special treatment just because he's the older child, it shouldn't be a problem, and your kids will likely follow suit.

Should you tell your twins who is older? We did from an early age, and it hasn't been a big deal. Now, granted, our girls aren't teenagers yet, but even with those mischievous toddler years that we've been through, it hasn't been a problem. Most twin parents I've talked to aren't afraid to tell their twins which one is older.

Good Twin, Bad Twin – Myth or Reality?

Occasionally I've been asked, "Which twin is the bad twin?" I never know quite how to handle this question. It is as if you must always have a good twin and a bad twin.

What does "good" or "bad" even mean here? Well behaved, as opposed to always mischievous?

In observing our twins' personalities and behaviors I don't see that we necessarily have a "good twin" and a "bad twin" all the time. The pattern I've seen is that each twin plays the part. And these parts are often opposites on purpose.

When one of our girls is having a fit or throwing a temper tantrum, the other all of a sudden is the angel child.

The "good twin" in this case will call out her behavior: "I not crying," or "I be good." The good twin is hungry for attention and wants to be praised for good behavior.

Here, as a parent, you have the choice. Do you focus on the "bad twin" to try to correct the behavior? Or do you pay attention to the "good twin" for proper behavior?

We've had success focusing on the "good twin." The "bad twin" starts to see this and wants the positive attention too. It has helped curtail some (but not all) bad behavior. After all, kids will still be kids and have episodes of craziness.

Parents of twins are blessed with all types of babies. You might have two "good" babies, two "bad" babies, or a mix. You can't predict what you'll get when you see that first ultrasound. However, you'll have your challenges any way you look at it. Other families you know will seem to have it easier than you do.

FROM YOUR FELLOW PARENTS OF TWINS…

"There is no such thing as a 'good' or 'bad' twin, and neither of them is easier to manage than the other. They seem to take turns sleeping or eating well. While one might be particularly grumpy one week, the other will take over the following week. They like to keep you guessing! Which of course leaves you at quite a loss when it comes to parenting — you have to constantly change your approach."

- Kim Lahner

Do your best with whatever temperament your twins have. Over time, you'll see trends in each of your twins and will know what to expect out of each. You'll be able to predict the behavior of your twins based on the situation and will learn what works to counteract negative behaviors.

CHAPTER EIGHT

Twin Gear

It seems that the baby gear companies are out to get every last penny from us parents. With twins, and perhaps pinched finances, you need to only get the gear that is best for your family. Don't listen to what the manufacturers and their advertisements say.

We loved finding slightly used baby gear at consignment shops or as hand-me-downs from friends. You'll use some items so little that it is a shame to buy it new and then so quickly have your twins outgrow it.

You've likely done most of your shopping or received gifts before the babies were born. Once your twins come home and start growing, you'll have a handful of baby gear needs that evolve.

FROM YOUR FELLOW PARENTS OF TWINS…

"For me, going into the pregnancy I knew how much 'stuff' babies needed, but what I didn't realize was how quickly the babies would go through the stuff! Infant bathtubs were only used for a number of months, maybe five or six months at the most. Things like bouncers and swings they outgrew just as fast. And for us, our boys got so big so quickly that they had outgrown their car carriers (and thus, their Snap n Go stroller) by six months old! It kills me how much money we could have spent on buying these items new, so I'm really glad that somewhere early on in our pregnancy I got the advice to get as much of that stuff used as I could stand. It saved us a ton of money in the long run on gear that was only used for a very, very short time."

- Corey Dalpee

Free Stuff for Twins

You can save a lot of money if you know where to shop and what you can get for free (or at least with a discount). There are actually a lot of stores out there that offer discounts and free stuff for twins if you follow their shopping promotions and keep an eye on store offers. If you live outside the United States, check your local options as those I list below might not be valid where you live.

Babies "R" Us, the infant and toddler branch of Toys "R" Us, offers a 10% discount on all big items purchased in stores that are intended for twins and multiples. You will have to indicate that you are buying for twins if you want to get the discount. Unfortunately, the 10% discount is only for larger items like car seats and furniture and not applicable for smaller items that cost less than $25. It is still a good choice for parents who want to save a few extra bucks. Babies "R" Us also gives you a gift card worth 10% of everything purchased on the registry. This could be a really healthy bonus if you and your wife buy things off the registry combined with what your friends and family buy. Make sure you double-check the fine print at the store.

Become a member of Enfamil Family Beginnings. Enfamil offers free baby products if you sign up right after your babies are born (you can inquire about it from your doctor) or you could give them a call to sign up for their membership network. This not only guarantees free stuff for twins but also lets you receive coupons that you can later use for discounted shopping. Sign up at www.enfamil.com/enrollment.

The First Years offers free toys for your twins or multiples. You'll just have to send them a copy of your twins' birth certificates and you'll qualify for their Multiple Birth Program. This is one of the best programs you can join if you want free stuff for twins and it is also a good way to get newsletters and other sources of good information on caring for twins or multiples. You can call The First Years at 1-800-704-8697 but will also need to provide more information via email or regular mail. Send an e-mail with the subject "Multiple Birth Program" to consumer@thefirstyears.com. In the e-mail, include your name, the names of your twins and their birthdays, address, phone number, and attach a scanned copy of their birth certificates. Alternatively, you can send this information by mail to The First Years Attention Multiples, 100 Technology Center Dr, Ste 2A Stoughton, MA 02072.

Call Beech Nut to get a special packet of discounts and some free samples for your twins. Call 1-800-233-2468 to make your request or go online to http://www.beechnut.com/contact/ and fill out the form with your name and address. In the message state that you have twins. You will be sent two New Parent packs that include coupons and free samples.

As a parent of twins, Gerber will give you coupons for discounts on their different lines of food products. Call 1-800-443-7237 to request a packet for parents of twins. You'll need to provide the twins' birth date.

The companies and business that are offering twin discounts and freebies is constantly changing. Make sure you review each company's offering to see if it can still serve your family.

See if you can get any free baby clothes or items from online classifieds and family members. Online classifieds such as Freecycle, eBay, and Craigslist can be absolutely indispensable for parents who are trying to manage the cost of having twins.

Remember to always ask for the twin discount. The worst that the store can say is "no." No harm, no foul. If you are dealing with a small business or local shop, there is always a chance that someone will empathize with your situation and that compassion may just drive them to give you a discount.

Since the time this book was published, some of these companies might have changed their policies and discounts. Always double check directly with the company to confirm your discount. You'll find an updated list of discounts and free stuff at www.dadsguidetotwins.com/more.

Fitting Car Seats in Your Car

As you discovered, you can't leave the hospital with your babies unless you have infant car seats. These baby carriers are great for latching into your car, carrying around (one in each arm to build up your muscles), or using with a matching stroller system.

Now that you've got the twins home, you might realize that the car seats aren't an ideal fit in the back seat. Twin car seats can be bulky. They might not fit perfectly in your car — like you have to slide your seat forward for them to fit. What should you do?

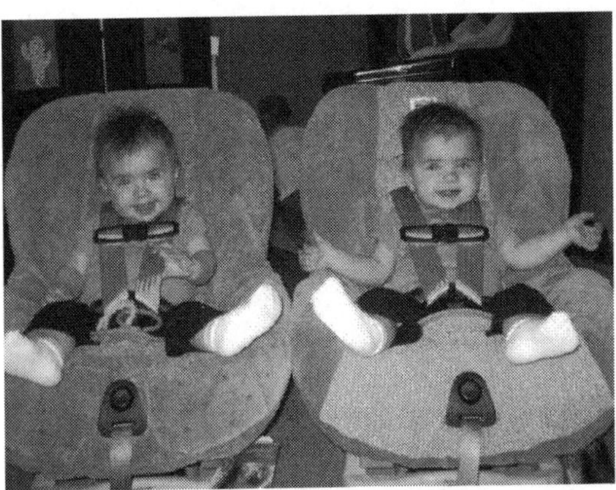

Bigger, convertible, post-infant carrier car seats

The first option is to wait it out as your twins will outgrow their infant car seats and need something bigger with different dimensions soon enough. This means you might be cramped if you have to move your seats forward to accommodate these seats. It's probably not ideal, but it is possible.

Option number two is to buy different car seats that actually fit in your car. You can do this by measuring the space that you have and consider buying a used or a hand-me-down car seat from a trusted friend or a family member that would fit better in the backseat of your car.

Option three is to buy a minivan. Minivans are designed to let people walk through that sliding door to get into the third row. Typically there's a lot more room between the driver seat and the first row of seats behind. The car seats don't butt up against the back of the chairs, and it is easier for others to get in and out of the third row backseat.

Depending on which option you choose, your choice will impact your budget differently. If you have no budget whatsoever, then stick with what you have. If you have a little bit of budget, maybe you consider buying different car seats that would fit better in the backseat of your car. If you know you're going to get a minivan eventually anyway, or you're going to grow your family some more, buying a new vehicle might be your best option.

Strolling Around with Twins

Although you might be tempted to channel your inner Arnold Schwarzenegger and carry your twins around in their infant carriers/car seats, you will eventually look for a more streamlined mode of transport for your twins, like strollers. In my first book, the "Dad's Guide to Twins," we talked at length about the different types of strollers for twins with the advantages to consider when making this purchase. As a quick recap, there are two major options for a twin stroller: inline and side-by-side.

Inline strollers are long and narrow and your twins sit one in front of the other like pilots in a fighter jet.

Side-by-side strollers sit your twins shoulder to shoulder across, both facing forward.

We started with a Snap-n-Go inline stroller that held our infant carriers. It's light, compact, easy to maneuver, and you never have to disturb a sleeping baby by taking him out of the car seat. Just lift the infant carrier out of the car, snap into the stroller base, and go.

Snap-n-Go Inline Stroller

When our girls reached about six months old, they outgrew the inline stroller because one girl could kick the other in the head. We then switched to a double umbrella stroller. Since these umbrella-type strollers don't need the bulky car seat carriers, they take up less space and aren't such a wide load problem.

Side-by-side Umbrella Stroller

You'll find a full list of top rated twin strollers at www.dadsguidetotwins.com/more.

Stroller Connectors: Make Your Own Twin Stroller

Your twins will need a stroller. If you already have an umbrella stroller (perhaps from another child) and don't want to buy a big twin stroller, you do have some options. Stroller connectors are the magic ingredient that can turn two ordinary umbrella strollers into a double twin stroller.

The advantage of using stroller connectors is that you can create a double umbrella stroller for a fraction of the cost of an official double stroller.

To make your own double umbrella stroller, you'll need two identical umbrella strollers and some stroller connectors.

These connectors work by attaching the two strollers together at multiple points. They firmly keep the same spacing between the strollers. This allows you to push both strollers without their wheels getting intertwined or having one stroller swerve off the path.

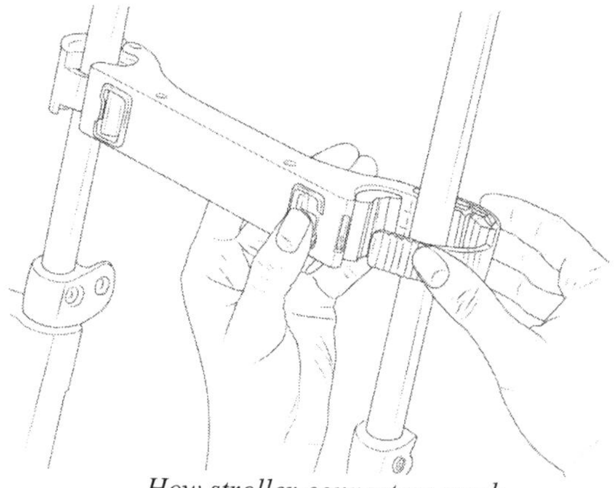

How stroller connectors work

There are only two major vendors that make stroller connectors: Prince Lionheart and Munchkin. Either will work great in many cases, assuming you have two of the same stroller that you are trying to connect. If you already have a stroller, try to buy another just like it. You could also buy two cheap umbrella strollers on sale for creating your own twin stroller.

The Prince Lionheart stroller connectors include three adapters made of sturdy plastic that link your two strollers together.

The Munchkin stroller connectors also have three adapters in the kit. They are easy to attach without tools.

From the discussions I've had with parents of twins, it seems that the Munchkin stroller connectors have consistently worked better than their Prince Lionheart counterparts.

Even if you buy a Prince Lionheart or Munchkin model, you may still need to modify it slightly to fit your strollers.

Alternatively, if you are engineer-minded, you could simply build your own stroller connectors. Remember that your twins' safety is your top priority. If your stroller connector breaks, you may have a runaway stroller with one of your precious babies aboard!

That said, you can probably mimic a connector that you buy with a short piece of wood or PVC pipe that you fasten to each stroller. If you are really short on cash, this might be an option. However, the pre-made connectors are so cheap ($10-$15) that you could easily get one from Amazon.com and save time and money.

Carrier for Twins: How to Wear Your Twins

Choosing a baby carrier for twins can be difficult. Not only are there many designs, but many are sold exclusively online because they are marketed to a smaller audience: parents of multiples. Because of that, you can't always try before you buy.

The first question to ask yourself is whether you'd like to have two individual baby carriers or one carrier meant for two babies. Both types exist to suit different needs.

If you are planning to use the carriers when both parents are present, such as on a family vacation, it may be best to have two individual carriers. We had two Bjorn carriers for just this reason. When one of us was alone with the twins, we'd prefer to put them in the stroller and not carry them on us.

One parent can carry one twin each in a Bjorn carrier.

If you want to carry both twins yourself, or if your spouse does, you'll need a double carrier for twins. This might help you keep both twins with you while you chase around an older child, for example.

Some carriers are more like a harness or a backpack for the babies. These include the Weego Twin, TwinTrexx, and the Maximom Baby Carrier. These designs have straps over your shoulders that connect to saddles for the babies. In general, this type of carrier is easy to get babies into and out of, though sometimes the straps and buckles can be confusing.

Another common type of carrier for twins is the sling style. These include the Moby Wrap and the Baby K'Tan. The idea here is to have a large piece of fabric that you wrap around yourself and your babies, keeping the twins close to your body. These slings are generally very comfortable to wear, but they are sometimes difficult to adjust and to get babies in and out of.

One advantage of the sling style is that one parent might even be able to wear two slings at once, depending on the design. The Double Take TwinSling uses just such a hybrid approach, with two adjustable slings held up by straps that you cross over your shoulders.

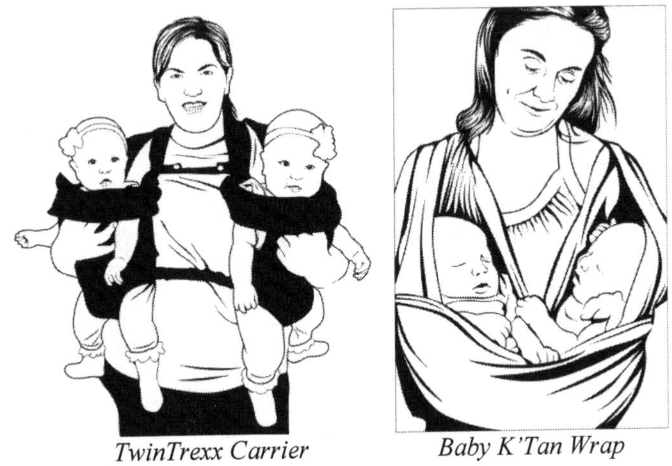

TwinTrexx Carrier *Baby K'Tan Wrap*

My experience is that the sling works great for newborns, up to about 3-5 months depending on the size and weight of your combined babies, and a harness carrier is better after that.

Pay attention to what weights the twin carrier supports. Some are made for very small babies, and others can accommodate your twins as they grow. Of course, you'll also have to consider whether you want to continue carrying your twins around as they begin to weigh 15 or 20 pounds (9 kg) each!

Many parents have raised the concern that babies could actually be harmed by carriers that suspend the child on a strip of cloth running between the legs like the Bjorn. These so-called "crotch danglers" are said to cause various problems, but the information I came across seemed to be more hearsay than anything else. If you are concerned, go straight to your pediatrician with questions rather than asking Google.

You'll find a list of the top rated twin carriers at www.dadsguidetotwins.com/more.

Pack 'n Play for Twins

Should you get a Pack 'n Play for twins? The answer depends on how and where you plan to use it. It is a Pack 'n *Play*, not a Pack n *Sleep*. It was intended originally as a contained play place rather than a crib.

Many parents will keep newborn twins in their master bedroom during the newborn months. If you choose to have the twins sleep in your room, having a full-size crib might not be practical. This is where a Pack 'n Play comes in handy.

Graco makes a special version of their famous Pack 'n Play that is specifically for twins. However, the reviews are mixed on this version, especially the twin bassinets that sit on the top of the frame.

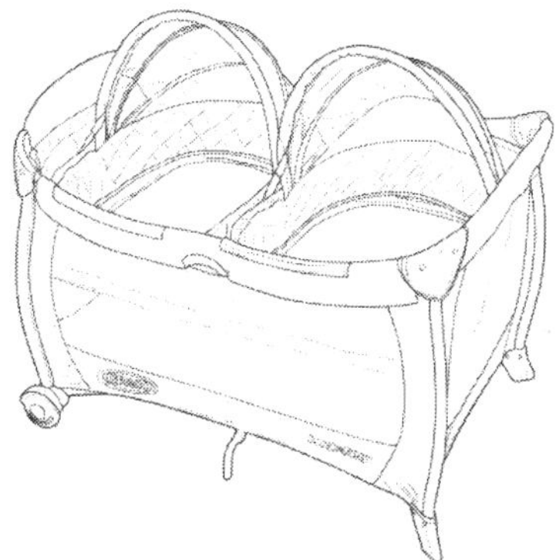

Pack 'n Play for Twins

You can likely get by with just a regular Pack 'n Play and skip the special Pack 'n Play for Twins version.

If you will be traveling with your twins, consider their sleeping arrangements while you are away from home. We had great success taking our Pack 'n Play on trips. Our girls shared the same one for sleeping on several trips when they were small.

There came a time when we needed to separate our twins during nap time. Having a Pack 'n Play in the house made nap time a lot easier. We could put one girl down for a nap in her crib and set the Pack 'n Play up in our room for the other girl. Having a dedicated Pack 'n Play for the twins' naptime was a huge convenience.

Do you need two Pack 'n Plays? We purchased two Pack 'n Plays for our twins — both on sale or at a low-cost consignment store but we rarely used both at the same time! We only needed one for nap separation and if we needed two while traveling, we'd borrow the other at our destination and only take one with us. Consider your situation and needs and see if you can't get by with just one.

Even though I've talked a lot about sleeping in Pack 'n Plays, they do also come in handy for actual playing. Put your twins in there when you need to contain them, or one twin, while you tend to something or someone else.

Toys For Twins

Despite what you might have heard, you don't need two of everything for your twins — especially toys. Even if you have identical twins, they are still going to have their own personality, and you aren't always going to want to get them the same toys. There are times when you will want to get them one toy to share, and other times when they will prefer distinctly different toys.

Newborn infants won't require many toys for the first couple of months. Having a mobile for each crib, however, can be a life saver, as oftentimes infants find the music and movement of the mobile soothing. Once they get a little older, then you can buy rattles and other chew toys and switch them between your twins. This way each child gets to play with the toy, but you only have to buy one.

If you are purchasing stuffed animals for your twins, they should each have their own, because babies tend to maul these types of toys to death. It is better to reserve the wipe-off toys for sharing.

There are some activity mats that are large enough for twins to use at the same time, and chances are once your babies are old enough to use one, they won't mind sharing. The same holds true of those ride-on toys for small toddlers. Different companies make two-seated versions of some ride-ons, which can save you a few bucks over buying two separate toys.

Of course, like any parent, you are going to want to teach your twins about sharing and cooperative play. You'll teach them to share not only with each other but also with other siblings and children as well, and there are plenty of toys that can accomplish that goal. Two-for-one easels offer a drawing pad on one side and a chalkboard on the other so two children can be creative at the same time.

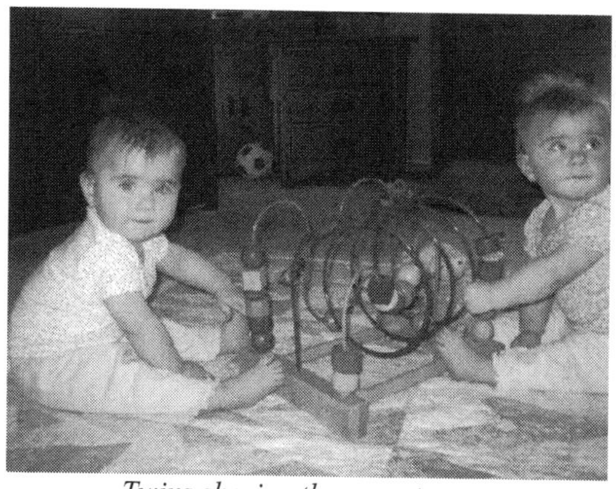

Twins sharing the same toy

A Noah's Ark is a great toy for twins as they can share the ark, but each child gets one of each animal. This toy encourages both imaginative and co-operative play. Teeter-totters are ideal toys for twins well.

As your twins get older they will be able to express their own individual interests themselves, but still will enjoy sharing games and toys with one another. Follow their lead, learn their interests and likes, and you won't go wrong when choosing toys for your twins as they get older.

Baby Monitor for Twins

Do you need two different baby monitors for twins?

It depends on how your twins are sleeping. If your twins share a room, they'll be fine with a single baby monitor in the room that will pick up any and all of the noises that are happening in that room. If each twin is in their own room, you might find two monitors helpful.

Having a baby monitor that only picks up sounds might be good enough to keep track of your kiddos. You'll find that your twins each make distinct and different types of cries and sounds that you'll learn over time and you'll be able to recognize which baby needs your attention just from a sound.

Several baby monitors are on the market with a video camera. I personally feel that video is a little overrated because you have to take the time to actually look at the monitor, whatever you're doing or wherever you are in the house, to see what's going on.

Audio is a much more efficient alert that lets you carry on with whatever you're doing in the house and will let you know when you are needed. It will interrupt you when something is happening. You'll hear your baby or babies crying and can take action.

Do Your Twins Share Clothes?

Once your twins move past just wearing onesies and diapers, clothing will become a bigger expense.

Our twin girls have shared clothing and still share to this day. You'll need to know how your twins will share clothes so you can plan your clothing purchases.

While twins can wear the same outfits, they can't both wear the same outfit at the same time. Yes, you still need multiple outfits. Nevertheless, your twins can take turns wearing the same clothing.

Obviously, it is easier for same gender twins to share clothes. Nevertheless, boy/girl twins can still share. The style and colors of the clothes will help guide your sharing decisions here.

When your boy/girl twins are infants it will be a lot easier to share the basic clothes that they wear every day.

Most of the recommendations below will work for same gender twins. However, if you're budget crunched or just haven't done all that twin laundry yet, I'm sure you can get creative.

Newborn twins are messy. They spit up, have diaper blowouts, and need frequent clothing changes. When you leave the house and want your twins to look cute, by all means dress them up. However, when you are at home, the reality of caring for them sets in. Fashion takes a back seat.

With all the messes and wardrobe changes, having your twins share a stack of onesies and diapers will be a lot easier to maintain than sorting out which clothing belongs to which twin.

During the first year, you (as the parent) will be choosing what your kids wear. You will also be dressing them each day. It is therefore your choice if they are to share clothes are not.

We color coded the clothing our girls wore to help identify them and so had distinct stacks of clothes for each girl. We opted for the higher maintenance method of sorting clothes in favor of early twin identification.

Once your twins start to talk and express their opinion, the clothes situation gets interesting. You lose control of what clothes are shared. Your kids will decide what they want to wear and will freely swap and share clothes as they see fit.

As the parent, you can buy clothing and say it is for both your twins. However, they will still receive clothing as gifts from family and friends. These gifts seem to hold a special place in their minds. Your twins will remember whose outfit is whose and who was the gift giver.

These gifted outfits may be shared but it often comes down to a negotiation between your twins.

As your twins get older, they will share differently. However, one constant is that sharing clothes is natural for twins, and you'll likely see it in your family, too.

Diaper Bags for Twins

Your twins need a lot of supplies when you leave the house. It can be a challenge to find a diaper bag that is a little manlier than the typical feminine patterns out there. Since there are more singletons born than twins, you might just find a diaper bag built for one, and most of the time that will be OK.

If you're only going out for a short trip to the store, a bag for a single baby will work just fine for twins. You just need to prioritize what you take and you'll be okay.

If you've got a change of clothes for each twin, some diapers, bottles, and pacifiers, you could probably stuff all that in a bag even if it's designed for a single baby.

If you're going on a longer trip, maybe a whole day outing to visit grandma, or to go to the zoo, a singleton diaper bag may or may not work effectively. You'll have to look and see how much of your stuff can fit in the single bag.

In our home, my wife made a custom diaper bag and it worked great for us. It wasn't a manly print — it had some nice floral patterns and bright colors, but you know, that's okay.

The Skip Hop Duo Deluxe Diaper Bag comes in a benign black and might suit your tastes.

One thing you may consider as an option is a backpack when you need to go out with the twins. We would turn our backpacks into diaper bags when we were traveling and they worked very well. It's easy to take them on the plane, easy to take them to the park, or to the zoo, and so on.

Ultimately, the style, the colors, or the functionality of your diaper bag won't really matter to others because they're going to be so focused on the twins and how cute they are, and how amazing they are, and then they'll start to pepper you with unwanted questions, none of which will have anything to do with the diaper bag you are carrying.

But whatever you end up choosing, please remember this one natural law: a big bag is a heavy bag. If you over pack, it will only take you once or twice before you learn how to pack lightly.

Should You Get Two Baby Swings or Just One

With twins, there is always the question of whether you need two of something. For some items, you do need two, such as two car seats. For others, such as a changing table, you can get by with just one.

We had only one gently used baby swing in our house that worked just great.

It seemed that we needed this swing the most when either my wife or I was alone with the twins. We needed a place to put one of the twins where they could be soothed by themselves and we could focus our attention on the other twin.

The swing was great for helping distract, soothe, and keep one child happy. You can use a swing to hold just one of the twins when it is time for a diaper change, feeding, or when you just don't have enough hands to take care of both twins at the same time. We found that having one swing was more than enough for our twins. In fact, we outgrew it after several months because we found that the twins weren't using it that much.

We used the two bouncy seats that we had a lot more than the swing. If you can only get your hands on one baby swing, that should be fine. You can find a good enough version from a family friend, at a local consignment, or thrift store.

How Many Clothes Dressers for Twins

As your twins grow, so will the amount of clothes they have. Where do you store all those outfits?

Since our twin girls share their clothes, we have a pile of shirts, a pile of pants, a pile of skirts, a pile of socks, (they each have their own pile of underwear) and they interchange those clothes every other day or however they see fit. If your twins are sharing clothes, you may get away with one dresser.

Boy/girl twins may have two completely different wardrobes. Once they start to mature, they need different places to store their clothes.

We used one dresser with our girls and, as they've gotten older, the clothes have gotten bigger. We still managed to keep one clothes dresser, but more and more of their dresses and their shirts get hung up in the closet, because they just don't fit in the dresser.

Keep in mind as the sizes of the clothes grow with your twins, you may run out of real estate quickly with just one dresser, particularly if you don't have a closet where you can hang up extra clothes.

If you don't currently have dressers and are thinking of them, consider a long-term investment in some furniture that you know you'll have for a long time. Remember that both children will eventually need their own dressers for their clothes.

When costs fall within your budget, go ahead and get two. If you currently do have a dresser or are making space for a hand-me-down or salvaged dresser, you can get away with one for now. You'll have about three or four years before your twins grow and their clothes get so big that they start taking up some serious space.

CHAPTER NINE

Caring for Twins

Often people wonder how hard it is to take care of twins. The best way to answer this query from others is to invite them over to help for 24 hours. Since you're right in the middle of this, you might even ask yourself, "Why do twins seem like more than one full-time job?" or "How am I going to have time to do everything with twins?"

Twins are more than a one-person job, especially during the first year. If you're in the thick of things with infant twins, it is completely natural to feel like you're overwhelmed and that you and your wife can't possibly get everything done. You can't. The twins need lots of care: feeding, changing, dressing, naps, sleeping, cleaning, laundry, and so on. The twins produce a lot of work.

We had to reset our expectations of what we could do and what we couldn't get done around the house. If you are trying to maintain everything that you were doing before twins, you need to start cutting back now, because that is not realistic. Twins are the new normal, and you need to adapt to the new reality of your family life.

You need to question every task, every activity, and every chore. Ask yourself, "What is the worst that could happen if I don't do this today? What's the worst that could happen if I don't do it this week? What's the worst that could happen if I never do this?"

When you start to question your routines or the things that are important and that you think must be done, you'll start to put them in perspective and realize that many things can wait for later.

Make a list of the most important things you need to do. They might not be what you think they are.

- Your top priority is the health of your twins. This means you must take care of them! Feed them. Help them sleep. Change their diapers. Keep them warm.
- Take care of mom's health. She will likely be caring for the babies around the clock. Mom needs to get rest and good nutrition to keep going.
- Dad's health is important. Yes, you need to eat properly and get some sleep, too, or you'll get sick and be useless.
- What comes next? Work. Errands. Chores around the house. For the first year with twins, the top three concerns will occupy most of your time.

During our first year with twins, we cut back on a lot of non-essential things. We had a messy house. We were less social with our friends and our family. We went out on fewer dates as a couple. We didn't do any home improvement or significant household projects during the first year with twins. In fact, my parents gifted me a lawn mowing service for the summer so I didn't have to mow the lawn (for which I was very grateful).

In the years since the first year, we've started doing all of those things again and gotten into a healthy routine of social activities, dating, and working around the house.

With infant twins, your focus should be on getting them into a predictable routine. Nap times and a regular bedtime will then start to give you windows of opportunity to get stuff done. Routines make it easier to look ahead and see the time that you will have to do something around the house, run an errand, go to the doctor's office, or to get something done for work.

If your kids are in an unpredictable pattern, you're going to feel like you're constantly trying to keep your head above the water. Work on getting them into a good and healthy routine that first year, and it will open up a lot of possibilities during the day that you never knew that you had.

As your twins get older, they will become more self-sufficient and you'll start to see a return to normalcy in your home.

Activities to Do With Both Twins Together

The logistics of caring for twins aren't easy. One question I get a lot is, "What activities can I do with both twins together and which can I do with only one twin at a time?"

The secret is that many activities can be done with both or separately. Generally speaking, taking care of one twin at a time is the easiest. This is what you can fall back to when everything is crazy. Take care of one twin at a time.

Reading time is great time with all your kids.

Activities to Do With Both Twins Together:

- Reading books
- Going for a walk
- Baths (once they are old enough to sit up)
- Feeding so they are on the same schedule

Activities to Do One-on-One:

- Getting dressed
- Infant baths
- Diaper changes (one parent shouldn't try to simultaneously change two diapers)
- Potty training
- Teaching how to eat

You will split your attention between both twins all the time. This is the reality of twins. You may all be engaged in the same activity but the twins must take turns of who gets direct parental attention.

When we started our twins on solid foods, we had both in their booster seats in the kitchen. My wife or I would sit in front of them to feed them. We'd give a spoon of food to one girl, then to the other, and continue this rotation – back and forth. So technically in the moment of feeding we were doing that activity one-on-one. However, it was also essentially all done at the same time with both twins.

You'll do many things together with your twins. But in these cases, they are things you'd do together as a family anyway, regardless of whether you had twins or just several children. Any type of family outing would fall into this bucket: errands, dinner, vacation, church, going to the park, etc.

If you wonder if something will work with both twins, try it. You'll quickly learn what needs to be done one at a time and what can be done together. This will change over time so don't give up on something forever just because it didn't work once. As your twins age, you'll be able to do more things together.

Time Saving Tips for Twins

Time is a scarce commodity with twins. Especially when your twins are young, they require so much attention and effort that time seems to be lost at every turn.

Here are some time saving tips for twins that will help you make the most of your day.

I'm a big advocate of a freezer meal shower when you're expecting twins. This will stock your freezer with food you can eat during bed rest and the early months with twins. The same principle is true with day-to-day living with twins. Keep a stash of ready-to-eat meals in the freezer that you can heat up when you have no other option. An easy way to do this is to make double of whatever you are already cooking for dinner. Freeze the leftovers.

When your twins are infants, make sure you've got a supply of milk or formula you can take with you on errands to help feeding time run smoothly.

Feed both babies at the same time. Don't let just mom handle all the care. If you help out, things go a lot faster.

Always keep your diaper bag stocked so you can just grab it and go when you need to leave the house.

Your mom asked you, and now you'll ask your kids every time before you leave the house, "Did you go to the bathroom?" A potty break at home will be twice as fast as one once you leave the house. Once you're out of the house, finding a bathroom and getting your twins to use it is a huge time waste.

When your twins are still in diapers, make sure they have fresh diapers before you venture out of the house. Unless you get a surprise poopy diaper, you should be fine until you get back home.

Keep extra diapers, supplies, and changes of clothes in the car. This will allow you to respond to any diaper blowouts or other incidents without having to go all the way home.

Save time by putting your supplies right where you'll need them. This could be around the house, in the car, or even at Grandma's house.

We changed a lot of diapers in the family room and not in the girls' room on their changing table. Because of this, we put a small supply of diapers and wipes in a basket kept out where we used them the most.

Look at your twins' schedule and see when the twins sleep and eat. You can avoid cranky babies by taking outings and errands when they won't interrupt or delay typical feeding and nap times.

Don't worry about folding baby clothes. Have a drawer or basket for each type of clothing (shirts, onesies, pants, pajamas, etc.) that you can just grab from and put on your twins.

It is OK to leave your twins in their pajamas all day if you're not going anywhere.

Bathe your twins together at the same time.

After the kids go to sleep at night, prep the house for the next day so everything is ready when you wake up.

When you try to care for twins one at a time, it will seem like you are taking care of the twins all day long. Try to split tasks between parents to make life a little easier.

Why you need a daily log for your twins

You may think you have a good memory, but you don't. (Or won't, in the near future!)

You don't have a good memory because of two things: sleep deprivation and twins.

During the early days of having your twins home, you will be so tired that you won't trust yourself to remember anything important. Unfortunately, you are responsible for something important: keeping your twins alive. It is therefore imperative that you keep a log of what is happening with your twins: feedings, diaper changes, medications (if applicable), amount of sleep and time of day, etc.

Why? Because you will forget.

You'll forget who ate last.

You'll forget who pooped and when.

You'll forget what time you put the twins down for a nap.

You'll forget when it is time to feed the babies again.

The solution: write it down. Instead of having to remember everything in your tired head (which you won't), follow this one easy rule:

Write it down.

Simple. You can make your own twin log or use an app on your phone.

After several weeks and when the kiddos start growing and settle into a routine, it won't be so much of an issue. But at the start, keep your sanity, keep your twins alive, keep a log.

You can download a sample daily log for your twins at www.dadsguidetotwins.com/more.

Organizing for Different Size Twins

If you've got boy/girl twins or even different sized twins, you'll need a systematic way to organize the nursery and diaper bag to best serve both kids.

Using different color clothes will help family and friends match the right size to the right baby. Of course, this will require that you purchase some new clothes or sort out the clothes that you already have if you're going to use color schemes on each of the babies.

Avoid writing on the clothes label. You may be tempted to put the name of one baby on one shirt and the other baby's name on the other shirt. Avoid writing on the clothes label unless you are sure you're not going to be passing these down to the smaller twin. The bigger twin is going to outgrow a certain outfit that you may want to pass down to the other twin. You don't want to have permanent markings on those clothes that would mess up your system later.

If you're using disposable diapers, you could label the diapers with a permanent marker to help organize your diaper bag. Additionally, you could use different brands or styles of diapers for each child. Maybe one's diapers are Pampers and the others are Huggies. Or maybe one is Elmo diapers and the other one is Cookie Monster diapers. Most diapers have their size printed on them somewhere but labeling them yourself will help you find what you need faster.

Have a clearly labeled basket in the nursery for each child with their clean diapers in it. Having a laundry hamper for each twin and also washing their clothes separately will help keep everything in order.

Get a gallon-size zip top bag for each twin with their name on it for use in the diaper bag. You can fill one with diapers and a change of clothes for each twin. That way, at a glance, you can reach in and grab the right bag or your family and friends can help you.

Remember to keep a camera handy for the times family and friends dress the bigger twin in the smaller twin's clothes because, despite the best system you have, they'll still get mixed up occasionally.

How to Give Twins a Bath

Since our girls are identical, we started with a rule in our home: only one naked baby at a time. This helped us keep them straight until we could tell them apart more easily and not have to rely on our clothing color-coding system.

Once our girls got mobile, they wouldn't take turns with bath time. They both wanted to take a bath and they both wanted it now.

Here are some tips I've learned about bathing twins in the bathtub:

- Get all your towels and wash rags ready before you start the water.
- Make sure your soap is within reach of your kneeling on the floor position.
- Put down a non-stick mat that covers the bathtub floor.
- Have a cup for rinsing the babies. You may need two cups so that one baby can play while the other is cleaned.
- Strip down both babies to their diapers so you can pull one's diaper off, put the baby in the tub, and then immediately take off the other baby's diaper in rapid succession.
- Once the water starts in the tub, you can't leave. Your babies will need constant supervision.
- Use the kneeling pads used by gardeners (you can find them at a garden center) while kneeling on the hard bathroom floor.
- You'll need an extra towel to mop up all the splashes.
- You'll have at least one twin that wants to drink the bath water. This same twin will then be surprised when too much water comes out of the cup.
- Be ready at a moment's notice to help a baby who slipped to sit back upright.
- Babies are really slippery when wet. Try to keep at least two points of contact when moving them.
- If you can get your spouse to help, you'll be a happier person. My wife would take a baby to dry off while I finished cleaning the other.

Do You Bathe Your Twin Infants Together?

We didn't bathe our twins together in the bathtub until they could both sit up by themselves. I tried, when they were just learning to sit up, and we just had too much trouble, because they kept slipping, sliding and falling down. It was hard to manage both of them at the same time and to keep them both safe and happy in the tub.

When our twins were younger and I was alone with them for the bedtime routine, I tried bathing our girls together and I also bathed them separately. It really depended on how old they were. When our twins were very young, I'd bathe them one at a time. I'd keep the non-bathing twin in a bouncy seat or sitting by me outside of the bath tub while I washed her sister and got her cleaned up. When it would come time to dry one of the twins off, I would make sure that

I didn't leave the bathroom. I'd take one twin out of the tub, dry her off, get her dressed in her pajamas, and then put her in the bouncy seat or sit her on the floor and she could play with some toys while I would wash up her sister. You definitely don't want to leave any of your children unattended in the bathroom, particularly when they're very young and when there's water in the bathtub.

By the time your twins are 6-9 months old you should be able to bathe them at the same time. The trick is that you have to keep your eye on both of them while they are in the bathtub. Like I said, little kids are extremely slippery when wet and you don't want one of them slipping under the water and having trouble. Just because a twin may be confident sitting up doesn't mean that he is going to stay up. Even when they can sit up by themselves on the carpet or on the floor, they're still going to slip around in the bathtub.

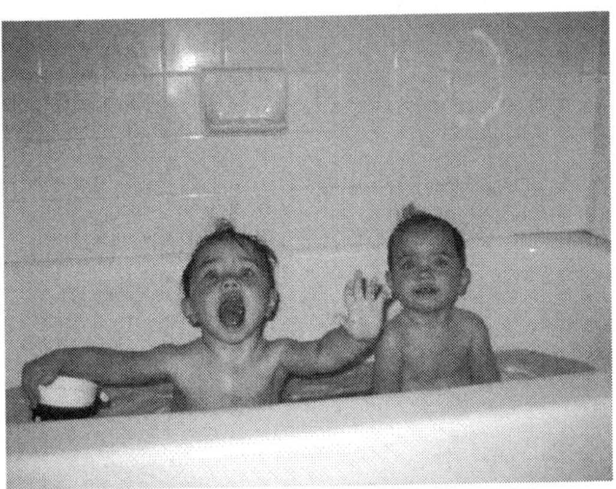

Bath time with twins is always exciting

When I would bathe our girls together, at the end of bath time, I would drain the tub while the twins were still in it to help make it easy to get them out and dry them off without having any extra slipping or underwater episodes.

Most babies love bath time. Keep a camera nearby because it is likely there will be lots of cute moments you'll want to capture while your twins splash around. If you want to bathe your twins together before they are totally independent in their ability to sit up on their own in the bathtub, then you might just need to have both mom and dad help with bath time. This will make it easier for you to clean them, to keep them safe, and keep them happy. The other advantage is both parents get to help with bath time, which is always a fun time for parents.

How Often Do You Give Your Infant Twins A Bath?

Once your twins are home from the hospital, you've got to keep them clean. Luckily, since infant twins typically aren't running around the muddy backyard, your cleanup efforts are predictable and routine for the first several months.

How often should you give your infant twins a bath?

The simple answer is: when your twins need a bath.

The reality answer is: when you can.

When our girls were born, we thought we'd bathe them every night before bed. The reality of caring for newborn twins made bath time a lower priority.

During the early months, most of your energy is spent getting your twins to eat and sleep. Bath time then becomes an inconvenience if you don't plan for it.

You should be fine bathing your twins every other day. Of course, they will have diapers leak (or explode) and those messes, while possible to clean up with wet wipes, will merit a bath sooner rather than later.

Who says that bath time has to be at night before bed? You can bathe your twins when you find the time. This could be in the morning or middle of the day.

Keep in mind that bath time will eventually become part of an important routine in your twins' daily lives. We like to include bath time in our twins' bedtime routine, but you'll find what works best for you in establishing a routine for your family.

With this in mind, start being consistent in bath time so your twins will know what to expect. In the early months this might not be as big a deal as later in the first year.

If your schedule is crazy, it is OK to bathe one twin today and the next twin tomorrow. We found however, that bath time was best done on the same night for both our girls. All the bath supplies were out and we already had water in the tub so it was a little more efficient to bathe them one after another.

Don't worry too much if your twins don't get a bath for a few days. You've got so many other things to worry about that you shouldn't beat yourself up if you miss giving your twins a bath here and there. (The same holds true for you.)

Additionally, excessive bathing can dry out a baby's skin. A few times a week is plenty so long as you clean the dirty openings like face, neck, and diaper area between baths.

As you get used to life with twins, bath time will become a natural and regular part of the routine.

Handling Both Twin Infants at the Same Time

When you've got two babies to care for at the same exact time, what do you do?

If you're alone, you don't have to do everything simultaneously. You may think you do, but you don't. Almost every request that comes your way can be prioritized. One twin at a time. Take turns.

Triage is the word of the day. Hospitals triage patients to determine which person needs urgent attention. You must likewise triage your twins.

Assess the situation and see who really needs the most help right now. Take care of the most urgent need first. This is not necessarily the loudest twin.

Having some baby gear on hand for your twins will help support the logistics of handling both twins at the same time. If one of your twins needs immediate care, put the other in a rocker, bouncy seat, or even on a blanket on the floor. These assorted baby gear items are your extra hands when you're alone and taking care of the twins.

You don't have to do it alone. Invite your friends and family to visit and help with the twins. If you, dad, are working a lot, see if you have some room in your budget to hire a babysitter to help mom for a few hours a day with the twins.

Many things can be done with both twins. Feeding, bathing, tummy time, and more can involve both kids at the same time. However, in each of these situations, you can take turns and still manage one child at a time.

What about carrying two twins at the same time?

Pick up one and get her positioned on your shoulder or arm. Then reach and get baby No. 2. It will take some practice, but you'll get the hang of it. As a bonus, your arms will get a workout.

Triage. Take turns. Be flexible and you'll do great!

Do Twins Get Upset at the Same Time?

There are a few factors that help you know if your twins will both be upset at the same time.

Twins will both get upset if they are in the same place and expecting the same result but don't get that outcome. For example, if you make a "yucky dinner," both twins won't be happy — even if that "yucky dinner" is something you find perfectly delicious (like anything with vegetables).

If your family is headed to a park, museum, or something fun but have to cancel or change plans, expect two upset twins.

If you are doing something fun and announce that it's time for bed, you'll likely have two upset twins.

Sometimes one of our twins will follow the lead of the other. If one gets upset, the other will react likewise. If you see a similar pattern in your home, expect double trouble.

How have your twins reacted to things in the past? They will likely follow the same path again this time. You can use this to your advantage to either change the circumstance or react differently to your child.

FROM YOUR FELLOW PARENTS OF TWINS…

"The biggest surprise for my wife and I is the ability of one twin to emotionally feed off of the other twin. We have a daughter and son and it appears that each child is somehow connected with the other. On several occasions my daughter will cry if my son bumps his head or is teething and my son shows no emotion. As a result, they pretty much have the same schedule making parenting easier and difficult. It is easier in the sense that they both fall asleep and eat at the same time; however, when they are fussy it makes it so that my wife has to take our son and I have to console our daughter."

- Stephen Germond

Why It Is OK for Your Twins to Cry

According to the Mayo Clinic, on any given day, the average newborn cries for two to three hours[3].

So while you might want peace and quiet in your home, the reality is that babies cry. It is natural.

When you first get your twins home, it will seem like they are crying all the time.

---

3 http://www.mayoclinic.org/healthy-living/infant-and-toddler-health/in-depth/healthy-baby/art-20043859

Why? Because they are.

All newborns cry a lot. That is the only way they have to communicate with you. It is perfectly normal for your twins to cry.

Hungry? Cry.

Tired? Cry.

Wet or messy diaper? Cry.

When one is quiet, the other may very well be crying. So your perception is that the crying never stops.

You may be tempted to rush to soothe your babies. Take a moment and wait.

If you try to immediately soothe your twins every time they cry, you will wear yourself out and go crazy. It is natural for babies to cry. Don't expect complete silence in your house with twins.

Initially when your babies cry, you should assess why they are crying.

If you are using the EASY steps, you will learn to recognize the different types of cries quickly. Babies have their "I'm hungry" cry. Then there is the "I'm sleepy" or "I'm poopy" cry. Or even the "My arm is stuck in the crib slats" cry.

Listen to the cry, see why your baby is crying, then start to recognize the pattern.

You'll soon find yourself jumping out of your chair and running to the "My arm is stuck" cry versus waiting a few seconds to see if the "I'm tired" cry stops since she is already in bed.

Is your baby crying? Relax. Take a breath, assess the situation, and then take action.

How to Soothe Crying Twins

Before you can properly soothe your crying twins, you need to find out why they are crying. Is it time to eat? Are they tired? Do they need a diaper change? Are they hot? Cold?

Once you identify and fix the problem and they are still crying, you can move to the soothing stage.

One method that worked well for us to soothe our babies was the 5 “S” method discussed in Harvey Karp’s book "The Happiest Baby on the Block.”

The 5 S’s are: suck, swaddle, side/stomach, shushing, and sway/swinging.

Suck: We used a pacifier for our newborns to help soothe their crying. Often, just inserting the pacifier into their mouths would calm our crying babies.

Swaddle: You’ll notice that the nurses at the hospital always swaddle up your babies in a tight little bundle. Swaddling helps keep your babies comfortable, warm, and under control. When our babies were crying, the first thing I’d always do (after the pacifier) was to swaddle them up. Swaddling helped control the flailing arms and legs that often accompanied crying sessions.

Side / Stomach: Pick up the baby in a football type hold with child’s body supported by your arm and his head resting in your hand. Make sure the baby is resting on his side or stomach.

Shushing: Loudly, but not screaming, make a “shhhhh” sound like when you are telling someone to be quiet. Do so close to your baby. Remember, she just spent several months inside mommy’s tummy and heard the constant woosh-woosh of her mother’s heartbeat (as well as her sibling’s heart beat). It was loud in there! Recreating that ambient noise will relax your baby.

Sway / Swinging: With the child’s head in your hand, you can gently sway the baby back and forth. Again, this is trying to mimic the experience in the womb where the baby was in constant motion as the mother moved about. There is comfort and familiarity in motion for the baby.

When we used the 5 “S” method on our crying babies, it magically soothed them at least 90% of the time. Often our babies calmed down after only a few of the “S” steps.

The method for soothing two crying babies at once is the same. The question becomes who gets soothed first.

If you have helpers around (which I highly recommend), each of you can soothe a twin at the same time using the steps above.

If you are home alone, you will have to decide which baby you soothe first. In this case, try swaddling each baby and then picking them both up and proceeding with the shushing and swinging phases as you carry both twins around the house. You will become a pro at carrying both twins at the same time.

It may feel like both twins always want you to hold them or pick them up. In this case, make sure you are reinforcing the behavior you want long term. It is not sustainable to hold and rock your babies forever. If your twins are always wanting you to pick them up, I'd try to keep it as brief as possible. Soothe them and then put them back down. Or try to soothe them while they remain in their bouncy seat. There is a time and place for holding twins, but if you do it all the time, they will continue to expect that and it is a hard habit to break.

Although having two crying babies at the same time will be nerve racking and frustrating to you, try your best to stay calm. They aren’t mad at you, so don’t take it personally. Stick to the 5 “S” method and when your babies start to cry, fall back into the familiar routine. By having a systematic way to soothe your twins, you’ll do so more quickly and with less stress.

Leaving One Twin Crying While You Care for the Other

Both of your twins are crying. What do you do? Is it OK to leave one twin crying while you attend to the other?

Absolutely. It is perfectly fine to let one or both of your twins cry.

Don't freak out when both your twins are crying at the same time. Don't get upset or mad at your twins. They love you, they just can't tell you that yet.

Take a deep breath and relax. It is not the end of the world.

When you are home alone and caring for the twins, it isn't always possible to help both at the same time. It is easier and perfectly acceptable to help one twin at a time. In fact, with twins, it is almost a necessity to do things one at a time. So don't feel guilty about letting a crying baby wait for his or her sibling.

If you aren't sure how to assess the situation, pick up the loudest and most upset twin first.

If possible, try to help the other twin self-soothe. Give her a pacifier. Put her in a bouncy seat. Let her rock in a baby swing. Try a temporary soothe where you don't have to physically soothe that twin. This will free up your hands to aid the most distressed baby.

How Your Friends Can Help You Care for Your Twins

The early days with newborn twins are a physical, mental, and emotional challenge. You'd be wise to recruit some friends or family to come and help you during the early months with your twins.

What should you ask them to do? Anything you currently take for granted or where extra hands would make things easier.

1. Watching the Other Kids

Your older children may be (or feel) neglected when the twins arrive. Set up play dates for your kids with their friends. Recruit a friend or family member to take them to the play date so you don't have to leave the house with the twins.

2. Taking the Night Shift

The true test of how much your friends and family love you is whether they will take a turn with the babies overnight. Will they help feed the twins, change diapers, and get them back to bed when they wake up during the night?

The beauty of this service is that you can get a full night's sleep, which is a rare and precious commodity. Even just one night will make a big difference in your world!

3. Babysitting

You can't stay in your house forever. You'll need a mental break from the drag of your routine. Invite your friend to come babysit your twins while you and your wife go out on a date or even just for a walk around the block.

4. Helping with Doctor's Visits

Taking your twins to the doctor's office for well-baby checkups is a juggling act. You always need extra helping hands to get babies ready for measuring and examination. Plus you'll need to soothe them after any shots or uncomfortable examinations. If you're not able to go yourself, rally the troops to help your wife.

5. Hold the Babies

Who doesn't like to hold a little baby? They are so cute! Exactly. Recruit your friends to come over and hold your babies, soothe them, and while they are there they can be called on to help with other tasks.

6. Feed the Babies

Regardless of whether you bottle feed or breast feed your twins, it is hard to feed both by yourself. A helper can bottle feed one baby while you feed the other. A friend can help bring babies to and from mom for feeding and take care of burping and changing.

Your friends and family are hopefully willing to help you with your twins. You just need to ask for help. Reach out to them with specific things they can do and they will respond and come to your aid. If you ask for general "help" you'll never seem to get what you need.

Should I Hire Help?

There is a time between when dad goes back to work and mom is still on maternity leave where things are really tricky for one parent to handle the twins. You might ask, "Should I hire help for my wife?"

There isn't really a question around whether you need help. You can always use helping hands with your twins. When considering if you should hire help, think about who you have available to help you and whether you can afford to pay someone.

If you can recruit family or friends to assist you in those early weeks, that is the way to go. You'll get known and trusted people in your home and will likely not have to pay a dime.

However, getting family and friends to help isn't always possible. Perhaps you are far away from family or don't have friends who are available to help in the way that you need.

If you need to hire help for your twins, it might come in several different forms.

Consider part-time helpers. Just because you need help doesn't mean you need help all day, every day. Consider getting help for just a few hours a day. This will help relieve the pressure and might just be enough to be sufficient.

In this case you could hire a babysitter for few hours a day. This person could help with your babies or even give you a chance to take a nap.

Remember that the safety and well being of your family comes first. Only hire someone you know and can trust. If you don't know them already, make sure they come highly recommended. You may also consider checking with your local multiples club to see what other parents of twins and multiples have done to find childcare specifically for their twins.

It is OK to test-drive a caregiver with your twins to see if it is a good match. If not, move on to other options.

Full-Time Child Care for Twins

If both parents were working before twins, odds are at least one needs to return to work after their birth. When both parents must return to work, you'll need to find a good caregiver for your twins.

Consider whether you want in-home care or childcare at a facility. In-home care might be more affordable with twins and especially with 3 or more kids since you likely won't be paying a per child fee like at a day care center.

Day Care Away From Home

Day care at a facility is what most parents choose for their twins. Typical arrangements are that you drop the kids off on your way to work and pick them up at the end of the day. Be aware that day care facilities charge per child. This can be costly depending on where you live. As we discussed in Chapter 3, day care can cost upwards of $20,000 per year for both twins (about $400-$600/week). Although some may give you a multiple sibling enrollment deal, don't count on the discount being significant — probably no more than 15%.

In Home Care: Au Pair

An au pair is a live-in family assistant from a foreign country. Typically au pairs are young women ages 18 and up. You use an agency to find an au pair for your family. Once hired, you pay the agency a fee that includes the costs of getting the person to your home. The au pair lives with your family — typically in a spare bedroom. She would work normal work hours while you are away and have the evenings and weekends free. In addition to caring for the twins, she would be responsible for other household chores like laundry, cleaning, and meal preparation. Au pairs are typically cheaper than nannies but it might be harder to find one that has specific experience caring for twins. Au pairs can cost about $360 per week or more.

In Home Care: Nanny

A nanny is a person who helps with your children but typically lives at her own home. The type of nanny you need really depends on your working arrangements after the twins are born. If both parents are working, you'll need a daytime nanny to care for the twins while you are out of the house. If mom will be taking time off from work to stay home with the twins for a while, perhaps a nighttime nanny would be of the most benefit to you. That way the nanny can help relieve some of the burdens of caring for and feeding the twins at night so that you and your wife are not carrying that full burden yourselves.

Each nanny's pay varies and is typically negotiable up front. Expect to pay at least $15 per hour and up ($600/week) for a full time nanny.

Finding a Care Giver

It's a smart idea to get a referral when hiring a full time caregiver. Use your local multiples club to get started. Do a Google search for your town's multiples club, or mother of twins club, and you'll find one. You can also check out the National Organization of Mothers of Twins Clubs, the NOMOTC, and you can find a location close to you. Go there, ask for a referral for nannies, au pairs, or day care, and they'll give you something to start your search.

If you can't find a caregiver that has worked with twins, consider one that has cared for multiple young children before. If a caregiver has been able to handle very young children easily for other families, then it may be a good fit for you with your twins.

One question to consider is the length of time you want to use paid help. Do you want help for just the infant months with your twins, or do you want help with your twins as they move into the toddler stage as well? Considering how long they will be helping with your children will help you find a good fit.

You must do some kind of trial run with your twins and the caregiver. You don't want to just interview them in isolation without the kids present, because you want to get a feel for how she interacts with your twins and how your kids respond to her. Talk with your prospective candidate about how they would like that to happen.

Put all your agreements in a contract that both parties sign. This is the place to clarify pay, days off, roles and responsibilities, work hours, etc.

Download a list of questions to ask a potential full-time caregiver of your twins at www.dadsguidetotwins.com/more.

The Exact Number of Kids that are Easy to Care For

With twins, you feel like you are always busy, always have your hands full, and never seem to get a break.

If you have other children in addition to twins, you'll be busy from the time the kids wake up until they go to bed.

I discovered the secret formula that indicates how many kids are easy to manage at once. This equation is based on the number of kids you have:

Easy = number of kids – 1

In our case, we have four kids. When one is asleep or at grandma's house, life is easy.

If you have just the twins, and get a time when only one is in the house or awake, life seems like a piece of cake.

This formula also explains why you can magically handle all the kids you have in your family while the guy next door can't handle the only child they have.

Since you have twins, "easy" is having just one kid.

So remember the secret and enjoy those moments when you are down just one kid. Take a break and relax. You'll find the silence is odd and you'll miss the one that is giving you a break.

But don't worry, before you get too relaxed, you'll be back to a full house and have your hands full once more.

CHAPTER TEN

Raising Twins

Once you master the basics of keeping your twins alive (via feeding, sleeping, and changing diapers), you'll realize that you have to actually teach them. You have to do the hard stuff of actually being a parent. While not always as physically demanding, raising your twins to be responsible, value-centered, well-adjusted people is hard.

You'll need to adapt to the individual personalities and needs of each twin. This creates its own set of challenges. Every action you take reinforces your twins' behavior for better or for worse. This starts early and is definitely true during the Terrible Two's when you're juggling double the trouble.

To have more peace and happiness in your home, you need to have a good mindset. Being a successful father of twins requires perspective. How you choose to apply that perspective will greatly determine how your day goes.

No matter how hard your day or the challenges you face, you can always find joy in the love that your twins will show you. Cherish the hugs, kisses, playtime, and excited faces when you reappear at the house after a long day.

When you are home, you need to let the work stress and related mental baggage go. Turn your focus and attention to your kids and your family. Look around you and see what's going great with your kids. Enjoy those small moments with your twins that make it all worth it.

Infant Twins Are Fun to Take Out In Public

While it may feel like infant twins keep you stuck at home every day, the reality is that when you do go out in public, it is usually a noteworthy adventure.

Any trip you take to the store, church, or park will merit superstar status.

Carrying twins around, one in each arm, or pushing them in their twin stroller is a perfect way to get special treatment. People will open doors for you. Others will move out of your way. You may even be able to cut in line. Enjoy the special treatment.

Odds are you can go to the store without kids and no one even notices you. With twins, everyone (even a total stranger) is your friend and wants to ask you twenty questions about your twins. Be prepared for the same questions every time and especially ones that would seem none of their business. (For example, "Did you have in vitro?")

Most of the time you spend in public will be with people watching your every move. They are fascinated because you and your twins are an anomaly. There are two babies. There's a twin stroller. "Oh, how do they manage!"

Your mom probably told you that pointing was rude. Well, obviously there was some unwritten exemption for when you see twins. Don't be surprised to see people across the room smiling and pointing in your direction. Smile and wave back.

Twins have some magnetic power about them that attracts complete strangers and invites them to get a little too close to you and your babies. People will act like they are the twins' own grandparents and try to tickle or pinch your twins and make cooing baby noises at short range.

If you're not comfortable with this, be prepared to position yourself between your twins and their admirers.

Nothing makes a twin parent more proud than having dozens of people tell you how cute your twins are. Assuming that your twins are cute (they are, right?) you'll get public reminders of their beauty every time you go out in public.

While you can start a collection of stupid questions and insensitive comments you receive, the vast majority of people will admire your ability to care for twins. They will claim that they couldn't do it or even give you a "God Bless You" in parting.

It is nice to be verbally recognized for the challenge of having twins. Enjoy it. You deserve it!

FROM YOUR FELLOW PARENTS OF TWINS…

"When I walk with both of them in the stroller, for some reason everyone thinks there is only one baby in there. They always lean in to look at the one that they see, and then are surprised as they see the other baby. Once a waitress at a restaurant said, 'Table for five ... Oh, wait ... six!'"

- Andrey Goder

Do You Need to Be Equal With Your Twins?

We have a saying here in our house that "fair doesn't mean equal." The kids don't always like it when we say that, as it likely means they aren't getting what they want. As you parent your twins, you can be fair without being equal.

It is not always practical or possible to be equal with your twins. If you are struggling to be equal with your twins, consider first if you are being fair. Don't worry about forcing the issue if you are doing the best you can.

Your twins don't always need the same things to be equal, like clothes or toys, but sometimes they will demand equality in the form of attention and time with you. As you spend time growing in your parenting skills, you'll get a good feel for when fair doesn't mean equal and when equality is important.

FROM YOUR FELLOW PARENTS OF TWINS…

"Everything is a competition. Like the constant temper tantrums they have when one gets something and the other one has no chance of getting the same thing."

- Ryan Powell

What if One Twin Needs More Attention than the Other?

Should it be a concern if one of your babies needs more attention than the other, or you end up holding one more than the other? Is it important to make sure to split time evenly for development and bonding?

Don't worry too much about giving extra attention to one over the other. There will be plenty of time for one-on-one attention from you and your spouse as you care for your twins.

One of your twins may very well require more attention and care than the other. Perhaps one is colicky or has a very different disposition than his or her sibling. In this case, the physical attention needed to care for the baby will be different between the twins. Just be aware that this could be the case and consciously plan for one-on-one time with the other child. If you have a particularly needy twin, make sure you are also giving time and attention to the other.

Try to rotate which parent cares for which twin if you find yourself falling into a pattern where one parent always cares for a particular twin. This way you can spend time with each of your children and get to know them better. It also gives the parent who frequently cares for the needy twin a break.

Bonding with your children is really a two-way street. There are feelings that you have and there are feelings that your children have for you. Consider how you feel about the bonding experience. Do you feel like you're giving enough attention and time to each of your twins? If not, try to shake up your schedule and think about how you can better spend one-on-one time with each of your twins during the routines of the day. You will be able to find the time that you need to bond with each of your twins.

Favoritism When Raising Twins

The circumstances of having twins often highlights the differences between each child, and you might find yourself preferring one child over the other. Favoritism when raising twins is natural, but doesn't have to be a problem.

Time spent with each twin may lead to favoritism of one twin over the other. This may be because you spend disproportionate time with one or that you prefer the "easier" child over her sibling.

Comparisons are too easy when you've got twins. Avoid comparisons – especially when Child A is doing better than Child B. It is fine to compare each against milestone benchmarks, but don't dwell on the fact that one child is better than the other. Each twin is unique and will develop at his or her own pace – be that physically, mentally, or emotionally.

Even in the midst of chaos, there are still things that are going well and can be counted as blessings and positive characteristics of your twins. Avoid dwelling on the negative of each twin and focus on what is going right.

Spend one-on-one time with each child to help build a relationship with each twin and avoid favoritism. This time together will help you see what is great about each twin and encourage you to not play favorites.

Don't express preference out loud to your children or family members. This builds a negative cycle where something that is temporary could grow into a more permanent preference or perception. Discuss the challenges you are having with each child privately as a couple but be united in how you show your feelings to your children in their presence and around family and friends.

Express love to each twin, praise each child, and admire what is good in each. This will help you avoid picking favorites.

How to Teach Your Twins to Share

Your twins have shared the very basics of life since they shared nourishment from mother and very tight living quarters while in the womb.

Upon arrival, your twins will likely share feeding times, cribs, clothes, and toys. Out of necessity and circumstances, your twins have been sharing from the very beginning.

With twins in the house a big point of contention will be sharing.

The easy way for you as the parent would be to get two of everything. However, this surely won't work all the time and definitely doesn't build character. As we all know, your job as a dad, of course, is to "build character." Right?

The biggest thing that your twins will share is your time. You can't buy any more of this precious resource. You will have to split your attention between your little ones on many occasions. There are some things in life that your twins will always have to share, and your time is one of those things.

When your twins are nicely sharing, you smile and verbally praise your kids. You feel satisfied that they will turn out OK in the end. These blissful moments often end abruptly with fighting over the same toy.

If you're like me, you'll probably prefer the sharing to the fighting.

One trick we've found very helpful with our girls (and our other kids) is the turn timer. The turn timer is simply a kitchen egg timer.

When the kids argue over a toy, game, movie, time with mommy, the swing, etc., we pull out the turn timer and set expectations. "It is so-and-so's turn now. When the turn timer dings, it will be your turn."

We set the timer for a minute or two based on how long we think our child's attention span is.

We'll follow up starting the timer by asking the kid with the coveted item: "What happens when the timer dings?" and make sure they understand the turn-taking process.

Yes, your twins get plenty of opportunities to share between themselves and other siblings. However, they still need some help and structure to get them in the good habits you are helping them develop.

It does baffle me that the kids will often listen to a small kitchen timer instead of just being obedient when my wife or I ask them to do something. Oh, well. There is nothing wrong with some extra tools in the parenting toolbox. Try the turn timer the next time your kids need a little help sharing.

If taking turns isn't going as smoothly as you'd like, then try the old distraction technique. Say, "Hey, look at that!" or pull out another toy, delicious food item, or favorite story to distract the sad, I-didn't-get-what-I-wanted twin.

When your twins are young, their attention span is extremely short. This means two things: first, set the turn timer for a very short time. Second, don't be surprised if the item they were fighting over is discarded and your twins have moved on to something else rather quickly.

The good news about sharing is that typically, your twins will be sharing better and earlier when compared to other singletons their same age.

Using Positive Peer Pressure with Twins

A wonderful advantage of twins is built-in peer pressure. Be it good or bad, you'll find your twins mimicking or following each other.

If left unchecked, this can become a downward spiral of bad behavior. On the other hand, with some gentle guidance and praise, it can encourage good behavior.

Fortunately, you can leverage your twins individually to help the other do what you would like.

There is a very powerful psychological tool known as social proof. By nature, we like to go along with the crowd. It is safe and reassuring. Social proof is an effective tool irrespective of age.

Even from a very young age, your twins will look to each other to see what they should be doing.

Is one twin jumping on the bed? Social proof: it won't take long for the other to start jumping, too.

Is one twin playing with her food? Don't be surprised to see her sister making the same edible artwork on the kitchen table. It's just social proof.

It is fine to handle each twin one at a time. This is a key step in using positive peer pressure.

When one twin isn't doing what you'd like, try this:

1. Ignore the bad behavior. Don't react to it.

2. Turn to the other twin and immediately praise what she is doing well. Be sincere.

About 80% of the time when we try this, the “bad” twin will stop the bad behavior and try to mimic the “good” twin to get the same verbal or other praise, like a hug, a pat on the head, or a big smile. (For the other 20% of the time, there’s always re-directing their attention or even a classic time-out.)

Ignoring bad behavior and reinforcing good behavior isn’t a natural response but it works like magic. It is definitely worth practicing until it feels more spontaneous.

My wife and I have had great success using the principles in Dr. Glenn Latham’s book "The Power of Positive Parenting" in helping our kids learn to make good choices. It was in this book that we learned many tactics that have served us well even when our girls were still very young.

What to Do When the Twins Only Want One Parent

Sometimes your twins will gravitate towards one parent to the exclusion of the other. This can be disheartening as a parent because you feel rejected or unwanted.

I have noticed that this pattern seems to come and go in cycles. It’s not a constant occurrence with our daughters, and your kids, as well, will go through cycles. I’ve seen that even though both of our girls can be stubborn about something, usually one of them is a little less adamant than the other.

I’ll look for the level of enthusiasm in each of our twins and then I’ll focus my efforts on the least stubborn twin. In so doing, I’ll increase my chances of success by focusing on the child that is most likely to respond. If she’s less stubborn or not throwing a temper tantrum (even if it’s only a little bit less than her twin), she’s more likely to be persuaded to do something with me.

Once you get one twin to do something with dad, the other twin usually follows because you have a beautiful pattern of positive peer pressure.

You can also try something called the alternative close that salespeople use when they're trying to sell you something. Instead of asking you a yes or no question, the salesperson will give you choices and encourage you to pick one of the choices even if you don't want either one.

This would mean taking mommy off the list of options. For example, you would say to one of the twins, "Do you want daddy to help you brush your teeth or do you want to do that yourself?" Mommy's not even on the list of options and so your child will have to pick one or the other.

You can think of similar examples that you can use in other situations, whether it's putting them in the car, or bath time, or whatever the situation.

Look for something, however small it may be, that your twins do with you, or near you, or for you. In this case, you're looking to reinforce the positive behavior. Take that opportunity to praise your child verbally, with a hug, with an arm around the shoulder, or even get mom to comment on how nice it was to see your son or daughter playing with dad.

We've seen our kids gravitate toward positive reinforcement and it does change their behavior over time. **The trick is to be consistent in reinforcing the behavior that you want to see.** However small the good behavior is, praise that behavior, reinforce it, and your kids will follow suit.

How to Stop Twins From Biting Each Other

Biting is a challenge with any kid but particularly twins because they're usually playing together, or spending time together and it's much easier for them to want to reach out and bite each other.

When our twins would bite each other, someone else, or us, we would stop the behavior, verbally explain that biting was not acceptable (which was usually as simple as "No! We don't bite!"), and then redirect the offending twin into another activity. This worked okay for us as long as we were consistent in our enforcement.

Your twins are going to start to look for the limits of your discipline, and they'll start to challenge that. If you are consistent in the actions that you take as a parent to counteract their bad behavior, they'll start to seek attention in other ways.

Try to identify why your twins are biting in the first place. Are they teething? Do they want attention? Is it triggered by something that's happening in your home or the actions of others? Address the root cause instead of just the symptom of biting. When your child is caught in the act of biting another child, you have to stop that behavior. Biting is not acceptable and can clearly distress or injure the other child. But if you can get to the root cause, chances are the behavior will stop.

Even before our kids could talk, we taught them basic baby signs so they could express themselves a little bit. That helped us communicate with them much earlier than we would have otherwise. Teach your twins some basic baby signs so they can express when they want something, when they want more of something, or when they're done with something. It's going to help mitigate frustrations that they have in communicating and deter biting as well.

Encourage your twins to use their words (or baby signs) to express what they want, when they need help, or if someone is doing something that doesn't make them happy. With better communication comes better understanding and the need to bite goes away.

How to Keep Twins From Fighting

If your twins aren't fighting yet, just wait, and it'll start soon enough. Perhaps it is because they're always together, they're the same age, or have conflicting dispositions. They'll end up fighting one way or another. Here are a couple of things that you can try to help keep your twins' fighting to a minimum.

In the moment of a fight, calmly tell them that when they fight, they cannot be with each other. If they're doing something that's not appropriate, separate them and redirect them to other activities. Say, "When you fight (or when you hit/kick/etc.) you cannot be with us." Then separate them and move them to somewhere else.

As you take each child to a quieter spot, tell them that you are giving them a chance to cool off and calm down and that they can return to their activity (or a new one) when they can be with the family again by behaving well.

Don't just think about how to keep twins from fighting in the moment of fighting. You can prevent fighting before it begins through how you interact with your twins during the rest of the day. We've discussed using positive reinforcement already, but sibling rivalry is truly an area where you can practice these parenting skills. Try to catch them playing well together or behaving civilly. Praise that behavior. The more you do this, the more you'll realize that the incidence of fighting has decreased.

You can prevent fighting by not forcing your twins to do everything together. Make sure that they're allowed to have their own individual space and time and interest in activities.

Let them pursue their different hobbies or interests. For example, we put our twins in soccer together and one of our girls loved it and the other didn't. Our non-soccer player dropped out in favor of another activity. That was OK.

Don't pile unnecessary comparisons on your twins. Don't foster that feeling of comparison and who's better than the other because the twins will use that against each other in their fighting.

How can you stop your twins from fighting? In the moment, separate them, and set expectations. Before the fight begins, make sure you praise good behavior and encourage good situations where fighting won't be something that they get attention for. In the interim, look for ways to reduce triggers that can cause flare-ups.

FROM YOUR FELLOW PARENTS OF TWINS…

"The funniest thing is their interaction with one another. They can hold hands one minute and then start to hit each another the next!"

- Anthony Pappas

Your Twin Toddler Forecast: Twinadoes

Your toddler twins will put on a show that can only be described as "twinadoes."

Imagine the Tasmanian Devil from the Looney Tunes cartoons. He spins like crazy, leaving a wake of destruction in his path. Then, he takes a quick break, looks around and starts spinning again.

Now imagine your twins' smiling faces in that whirlwind of destruction and enjoying every minute of it. There is something magical about toddler twins that you won't see with a singleton toddler.

Your twins will run, jump, climb, topple, wrestle, destroy, demolish, slam, bite, hit, kick, cry, scream, and bounce off the walls like nothing you've ever seen.

The twins will feed off the actions and energy of the other to create super twinadoes that you'll be hard pressed to contain.

Your clean family room will be struck by the twinadoes and you'll have to carefully tread through the aftermath.

Yes, the twinadoes will even splatter food, spill drinks, leave crumbs, and dirty up your clean kitchen.

So don't get too hung up on keeping your house spotless and tidy. As long as you have twinadoes roaming your halls, you'll have messes to clean up.

The trick is to use the time when the calm eye of the storm is present to teach the whirling dervishes how to clean up their own messes!

How to Do Chores With Twins

When your kids are young, they love to help around the house. This is both a blessing and a curse. Yes, it is faster for you to do something yourself. However, you need to teach those kiddos how to work and train them to see what a properly completed job looks like. As soon as your kids hit the toddler stage, they are ready to help do at least simple chores.

When looking for chores or tasks that your twins can help with around the house, you'll need to come up with double the work. You don't want one twin to do everything while the other sits idle. The other one will probably be eager for her turn as well. Where possible, see if there are any tasks that can be done in tandem.

Having the twins both work on one thing or having each of them do a different task is an important part of learning how to contribute to the household. When you're having your kids help you do something, remember that it's not going to go as fast as if you had done it yourself. It's definitely not going to be done as well as if you had done it yourself. That's just part of the process.

It's OK to slow down to show them how to do a task and take time to help them do it themselves. You may have to supervise and manage as they do those tasks. Overall, it may take you longer to do something, but that's OK, because ultimately the kids will become more self-sufficient in those things, and eventually they will be able to do them on their own. That is when this investment of your time will pay off.

Example Job: Taking Out the Trash

A perfect job for twins is taking out the trash. There should be plenty of trashcans throughout your house that need to be emptied. Additionally, we (like many of you) have both a trash can and recycle bin. There's two things right there that each of your twins can help with. One can take out the trash and the other can take out the recycling.

Example Job: Yard Care

When your twins are a little bit older, they can help with mowing and trimming the grass. Until that time, things like pulling weeds, sweeping, or raking leaves are big hits with little kids. Somewhere between toddler and teenager, doing yard work becomes a burden and no longer fun to do. Take advantage of the early years when your twins are still enthusiastic to work outside.

Example Job: Watering

One thing our kids love to do is water the outdoor plants. Watering the garden, the flowers, the trees, the plants, the grass - you name it. Kids love water in general: in the bathtub, in the pool, at the beach, and in the backyard. Letting them take turns with watering and the hose is a great thing they can do in the afternoon in your backyard.

Remember that you can't just give assignments. You'll need to show and help perform many chores around the house alongside your kids until they are old enough to work independently.

How to Keep Your Twins from Whining All the Time

Some days it seems like your twins are whining ALL THE TIME. You're about to pull out your hair because this is driving you insane. It is unbearable as a parent to have to deal with incessant whining from your children.

When you have twins and they both start to whine at the same time, it really compounds and makes things worse. We struggle with this, too, in our house.

I'm thinking the whining we get from our girls right now when they're young is kind of foreshadowing what they're going to do when they're teenagers later.

We found success with our twins by pointing out when they start to whine. We say, "You don't get what you want when you whine and you cry." This has reinforced our expectations that we set with them.

As long as we don't give in to their whining demands, it seems to work. For example, we say, "Hey, you're not going to get what you want when you whine." And we don't actually get them what they want when they whine. They start to settle down when they see we are serious.

Another method that we've found helpful is to answer the initial request or question but then refer back to that on subsequent requests.

For example, when your child asks "Can I have a cookie?" and you reply, "No, you can't have a cookie," they likely won't stop there. They will ask again repeatedly for the cookie. Instead of again replying with, "No, you can't have a cookie!" and getting frustrated at repeating yourself, you need to establish a new standard for replying to repeat questions.

Ask your child, "Did I already answer the question about having a cookie?" Since you did, they will likely nod agreement. Next, add "Do I look like the kind of dad that will change my mind if you ask me over and over again?" Depending on the mood of your child, they might answer "yes" or "no" but your response the next time they ask for the cookie is, "Asked and answered." You're acknowledging your child's request, reminding them that you've already made a decision, and answered their question. Once this pattern has been established, all you'll need to say in the future is "Asked and answered!"[4]

It's imperative that you be consistent and don't give in to the whines. Otherwise, it's just going to reinforce that whining does work. And they just have to do it maybe longer or louder than they did before until they get you to cave.

---

4 http://www.positiveparentingsolutions.com/parenting/end-child-nagging-negotiating-with-just-three-simple-words

How to Survive the Twin Blame Game

As your twins get older, they will start to get into trouble and be more mischievous. Yes, it is true. They won't be little angel babies forever.

When any child does something wrong, there is usually a consequence. Something is broken, lost, or left undone. A common practice is that the child will blame a sibling. You likely saw this growing up in your family or with your other children before twins.

With twins, things get really interesting. Each child has an ever-present scapegoat. Someone who is the same size, similar appearance, and is easy to blame.

Your twins will blame each other. They will point fingers. They will deny any involvement. They will even implicate the other in whatever shenanigan is causing you to be angry.

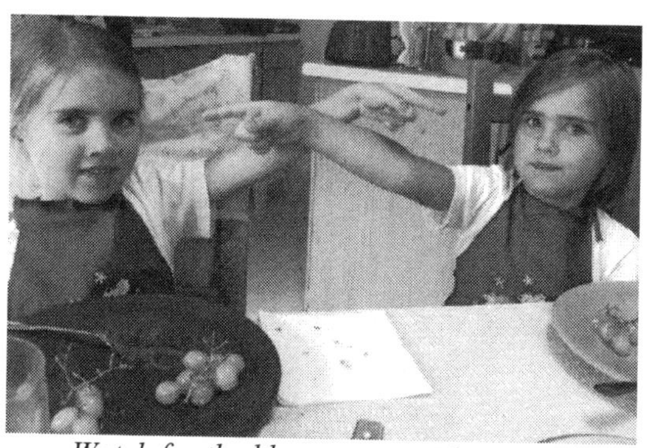

Watch for the blame game with your twins

As you observe your twins, you'll start to notice when one is lying or not. Call it parental intuition or just the innocence of youth making it painfully obvious something isn't the truth.

When you jump to the conclusion of which twin is the guilty party, look for the reaction of both twins. You'll start to see different reactions meaning, "I've been falsely accused" or "OK, I'm guilty."

Who is at fault doesn't really matter. Forgive, forget, and move on. No need to reinforce bad behavior by making a big deal about it. You're not out to prove who is at fault. Your job is to see that natural consequences are handled justly.

When in doubt, make your twins take turns cleaning up the mess that one of them made. This will quickly start to help them take responsibility for their actions.

Each of your twins will tend to do certain things that break the family rules or annoy you. You'll start to see patterns in what each of your twins does or doesn't do. These habits will be easy to spot. You'll catch a twin in the act of committing the crime. Or the scene will have telltale evidence of who was involved.

As a parent, you'll be able to know who did what even though you've got both twins blaming each other. Have patience and a discerning eye and you'll be able to survive the twin blame game.

How to Avoid Criticizing Your Twins

As fathers of twins, we have lots of challenges and physical demands that can weigh us down heavily.

There is one thing that we can do to help us plow through these challenges, and that is make sure that our mind is in the right spot. When our head is in the game, we can be successful as fathers of twins.

You need to be forgiving. Kids don't always do things on purpose, and you're probably finding this out as you interact with your twins. Sometimes they don't know what to do, they do something that is clumsy, or have an accident. Often their intention is not malicious, especially the younger the child is. If you want to teach your kids how to forgive others and understand the principle of forgiveness, you have to practice that yourself.

The same thing applies to your wife, especially during that first year when both of you are sleep deprived. Sleep deprivation wreaks havoc on your interactions with others and your ability to think straight. As such, your wife is going to do crazy things that maybe she didn't do before the twins arrived. You need to be forgiving of her mistakes.

You need to be understanding. Is one of your twins acting up? Try to understand the root cause of that. Ask yourself, "Why is my child acting up?" When they are younger, it may be a simple question of whether they have eaten, had their diaper changed, or are ready for a nap. Once you've diagnosed the root cause, it's easier to understand and then take action to correct the problem.

The same thing applies with your wife. If you get home after a long day of meetings and work, you need to be understanding of the situation when you arrive home. It's probably not going to be ideal, and you probably need to jump in and help anyway.

You'll have to do things yourself. Oftentimes you may want to blame your kids or your wife for not doing something that you think should have been done. In this case you need to step up and fill the gap around the house, and with the family, and with caring for your twins. You have a big responsibility in your family and your home, and if something isn't getting done, take care of it yourself and help teach your kids how to do that.

You need to think positively and look on the bright side of things. This will definitely help you be positive in the interactions with your family.

Avoid criticism at all costs. Frankly, criticism doesn't help any situation. It only makes things worse. If you have a tendency to criticize your kids for what they did, or didn't do, or the performance they rendered, or the quality of their work, stop. Do not criticize.

Things that your twins do on a consistent basis may trigger a negative behavior or a negative habit from you. You can choose to change those habits. Identify what they are first, and then see what is triggering those bad habits. Then you can substitute those with a good habit, something that you want to have happen. Then you need to practice. Every time one of your twins triggers a bad habit of yours, or a bad response from you, change that response consciously to something else. Over time it will become easier and easier to do.

Teaching Your Twins How to Swim

The most important thing to remember while taking your twins swimming is to be safe. This means that your personal enjoyment takes second place to the safety of your kids.

You are the lifeguard for your children when you are at the pool – especially when they are very young. Don't forget that responsibility, even if there is an official lifeguard where you are swimming.

As with many things with your twins, you don't always have to do everything at the same time.

When your twins first start to learn to swim, you can teach them one at a time. If you're lucky and have your spouse with you, you can each take a twin and work with them in the water.

Our twins used ring floats, life vests, and arm floaties for many summers as they started to master swimming.

We took advantage of swimming lessons at our local community pool for several summers. They had classes for different ages and skill levels. Look for similar opportunities where you live.

After the class is over (our classes were two week sessions), practice what your kids learned with them. By reinforcing the skills they have learned and getting them more comfortable in the water, they will make much faster progress than if you left all the training to just the swim instructor.

We've seen success taking turns helping each of our girls while the other watches. For example, my wife will help one daughter with her swimming strokes and kicks while the other daughter sits on the steps and plays (or watches). It helps if you tell them you're going to pretend to be at swimming lessons!

Just like many things with your twins, they will each learn to swim at different paces. You may likely have one child who is like a fish – swimming effortlessly from the start. The other sibling may be terrified of the water. Maybe one is more comfortable floating on her back and the other excels at swimming strokes while on her belly. Tailor your time in the water to each child's unique needs. Build on their respective strengths and be patient.

Swimming with your twins is fun but make sure they have a safe time in the water too.

College Savings Plans for Twins

If you want to your twins to go to college, now is a great time to start saving for that expense. While you likely won't be able to think straight for several months after the twins are born, the reality of compounding interest in your favor may compel you to start saving sooner rather than later.

The first thing to keep in mind is that you will need to take care of yourself and your wife first, especially as you prepare for future years of retirement. Your kids can always work or get a scholarship for college. However, you cannot get a scholarship for retirement. If you have to decide whether you need to save for college or for retirement, definitely focus on retirement savings for yourself first and then college second.

Try to set up an automatic savings plan every month based on your budget. This will help make sure that you're putting away some money over time for the future expenses that your children will incur. You'll need to examine your budget to see just how much you can set aside for that purpose.

One of the questions you may have is, "How will I even know if my twins want to go to college when the time comes?" If you're not sure what the future will bring for them, it's OK to save money anyway outside of an official education-type restricted account.

For specific financial advice on 529 plans and saving for college, I highly recommend you consult a financial advisor who can tailor advice specifically to your situation.

Once your twins are old enough for an allowance, make sure that they are saving a percentage of it for the future. You can talk about the future however you like. Maybe you encourage them to save this money for college, or it could be some other future goal that's several years away.

We do this with our kids, and have since we started their allowance, even from a very young age. When they get their allowance, they know certain coins are going to go in certain parts of their piggy bank, which has different slots for future savings, for fun money, and for charitable contributions. It's become a habit for them, and they don't even question the amount that goes into each of those buckets, and they're happy to do all those things.

We talk with them frequently about the purpose of charitable giving as well as saving for the future, whatever it holds for them.

Even though they are getting a relatively small amount of allowance because they are still little children, it will help establish that pattern, so that when they start to make more money with future allowance or when they start to get a job when they are older, they will still have the habit of saving and allocating their money responsibly.

CHAPTER ELEVEN

The Other Kids

Difference Between Parenting Twins and Just One Child

When our girls were born, we already had two boys. Due to this past experience, we noticed there were some differences parenting two versus just one child.

Sleep Deprivation

One of the big differences I noticed was that there's really no rest for dad or for mom with twins. When our singleton boys were born, my wife breastfed them and thus took the brunt of the work feeding and caring for them, especially overnight. Whereas when our twin girls were born, we ended up bottle feeding, and that required that both of us were on duty all the time to help feed and care for our girls. Intense sleep deprivation was a huge difference from the dad's perspective with our twin girls versus our singletons. Poor mom is going to be sleep deprived either way but it is definitely worse with twins because there's more work to be done.

Twin Infants Need Both Parents

Another big difference that we noticed is that both parents are required for basic child care with twins. This includes everything from feeding them, changing them, helping them get to sleep, to soothing them. That's going to require all hands on deck. It's very difficult to take care of even the basic needs of both twins with just one person. If you were not as involved with the care of a previous singleton child before, that's not going to cut it with twins. You're going to have to get involved. You're going to have to roll up your sleeves and get to work.

Divided Attention

You have divided attention with twins. With one infant, you can spend all the time that you need with him or her. Be prepared to be distracted and have your attention divided with twin infants. One twin is going to need something and almost at the same exact time the other twin is going to need attention as well. That's just not the case when you have a singleton baby.

Twins Require More Resources

Twins require an insane amount of diapers and laundry. Any new baby is going to have a lot of diapers and a lot of laundry because they're going to soil themselves, spill on themselves, spit up, blow out their diapers — you name it. It seemed like it wasn't just double diapers and double laundry, it seemed like a whole lot more than that. Be prepared for a lot more maintenance around the care of your babies than you may have seen with a singleton baby.

With a singleton child, you feed the baby and then you move on to other things, change the diaper, put the baby down for nap, and away you go. With twins, the pattern's the same. You feed, maybe have some activity time, change them, and put them down for nap or for sleep and then you repeat the cycle. However, with twins you need to make sure that they stay on the same schedule. Otherwise, things are going to get really crazy, and you want to make sure that mom is able to take a break between feedings.

Twins Need Special Parenting

With twins, you also need to force yourself to treat them as individuals and not as "the twins." Don't group them together; don't necessarily assume that they're going to be the same, because they are unique and distinct even though they may look exactly the same. Pay attention to their individual characteristics and personalities and focus on what makes them unique and amazing.

With a singleton child, you don't necessarily have to look for those differences because you have just one baby, and you can focus all your attention on that one child. With twins, it is very hard to give them one-on-one time, unless you make that a priority.

Focus on building a special bond with each of your children individually. Don't always do everything with both of them. You want to build and create individual memories and experiences with each of them. Of course, with a singleton child that's not really a problem because it's just you and your baby.

Twins Interact in Their Own Ways

Twins do have a natural bond with each other. It's very interesting to observe their interactions with each other and how they play off each other's emotions, habits, and activities. Our girls are best friends and they do everything together throughout the day. With a singleton child you're not going to have a built-in playmate, associate, or a partner-in-crime as you will as a twin.

Intense Moments and Seasons

A big challenge of twins is that they will go through the same stages of life at the same time. Big milestones like crawling, walking, potty training, learning how to eat solid foods, and teething are going to happen around the same time. You don't have the luxury as you would with a singleton child or a sequence of singleton children of practicing and learning as you go along. This means that there is more pressure to get it right the first time. Yes, there will be trial and error, but do the best you can.

Negative Influences

Twins play off each other's mischievous natures. They will get in trouble together often. In fact, if one twin gets into trouble, he or she will pull the other twin into the mix to get them into trouble as well, because trouble oftentimes is very fun to little twins. Trouble doesn't seem to escalate as quickly with just one child.

What You'll Experience

There are a lot of differences between singleton babies and twin babies. There are a lot of experiences that you will have as a parent in those first few months with infants and as they continue to grow. The differences in pregnancies from a singleton to twin pregnancy foreshadow the fact that you're going to have a very different parenting experience with twins than you do with a singleton child.

FROM YOUR FELLOW PARENTS OF TWINS…

"I knew it would be more work. My friends who had twins told me as much. But my wife and I were blown down by just how much more work twins are than singletons. This changed our approach to lowering our ideals to just above survival status!"

\- *David Gunn*

How to Handle Older Children After Twins Arrive

If you've prepared your older children for the arrival of twins, you've made good progress. However, your work is not done. You need to actively manage your relationship with your older children and be attentive to their needs even when you have your hands full with newborn twins.

You should have regular conversations with your older children about how things are changing around the home and with the family. Reiterate that you still love them very much and that you care for them. They need to know that they are still an important part of your family even with the new arrivals. Your other kids need to know and appreciate that you need their help around the house and with the babies.

You may be worried that your older kids feel left out or unloved. Since you do love them, the trick is to show that and involve them so they still feel it. You can help them with this adjustment to having twin siblings.

One-on-One Time

Your life can very easily be consumed by sleep deprivation and taking care of the newborn twins. You need to consciously make plans to spend time with your other children.

I took advantage of the twins' naptime to play with my boys or take them out of the house for some activities. My wife would take advantage of quiet moments to read to the boys. We tried to make it a point to eat meals together as a family so we could talk with the boys about their day, even if it meant their sisters were in their bouncy seats on the kitchen floor.

Schedule time specifically to spend one-on-one time with your older children. This way, the busyness of life and work doesn't crowd out the need to spend individual time with your children. I think it's very important that you are consciously aware that this may be a challenge and therefore you will be looking for opportunities to spend time with each of your children.

Try to Maintain the Schedule

Once the babies arrive, your schedule will be turned upside down. To help keep some normalcy in the life of your other kids, do your best to keep their routine as it was pre-twins.

Just like before our girls were born, I'd help give our boys baths and get them ready for bed. With so much change in their lives, having something constant was a big help. We tried to maintain the routine that was familiar and important to our sons so they could have a sense of security and comfort amidst the change.

Look for Kid's Reactions

You have doubtless heard tales of older siblings not coping well with the new babies. They may act out, start hitting, throw tantrums, or fight. Be aware that there is no prescribed timetable for this to happen. They may be fine initially, and you may be tempted to boast about how well they're taking the change. Keep a weather eye out. This may be because they are getting extra attention from a visiting Grandma, or because the twins are still a novelty.

The big change will eventually catch up to them and you will see behavioral changes. Don't be surprised if you see some regression in their behaviors. This may include steps backwards with potty training, speech, or sleeping.

Do your best to see their behavior for what it really is and be ready to dole out extra hugs, snuggles, and kisses. Your child still needs to know that they are important to you.

No Big Changes

Bringing twins home is a big enough change for your other kids. Don't add to the mix with other changes. For example, don't start potty training or move your older child out of a crib around the same time that twins arrive.

We had our boys move rooms several months ahead of our due date and let our youngest boy stay in his crib. We bought a new crib (since we were going to need two eventually, anyway) and kept the twins in the new crib together for a few months. When it became evident that each girl needed her own bed, we had our son give up his crib to his sisters and moved him to a big boy bed. By then, we had fallen into a good rhythm with the new family dynamics so the change was less traumatic for our youngest son.

Take Care of All Your Kids

No matter how busy you are, how sleep deprived you get, or how much your twins need attention, you must remember that you have other kids, too. Even small gestures will help them feel loved. Talk to them. Sit with them. Play with them. Have them help you with tasks that need to be done anyway but will help them feel like they're important to you.

It may be hard for you to fathom the possibility that you might be able to love two more babies. All the clichés are true. You will find that your capacity to love your children grows with each child.

If you have a close relationship with a child and you're worried that these new little beings will mess that up, take heart. The relationship you've nurtured with your child has only prepared you to do the same with your twins.

Make time for all of your kids. The new reality will fade and life will go on, but what you're left with are the relationships and memories that you've cared enough to take time for and nurture.

FROM YOUR FELLOW PARENTS OF TWINS…

"Our babies, like others, were born with very tiny white spots (called milia) on their faces. Our adorable nephew Cristian innocently asked when he met his new cousins for the first time, "Are those sugar sprinkles on the babies' faces?" Our family was so happy to see that Cristian was so accepting and excited in his new role of big cousin to his new two best friends."

- Brian Zufolo

Getting Older Kids Settled

When you've got older kids running around the house, you'll find it difficult to get them settled down for bed so you can tend to the twins. From dinner time all the way to bedtime is the craziest time of day. That's when the kids seem full of energy, when mom and dad are worn out from a long day, and you need to get the kids fed, bathed, and in their pajamas for bed.

One thing you can do is divide and conquer. You can take the older kids and your wife can handle the twins, or vice versa. Or maybe you both get the twins down and then spend time with your other kid(s). Try different things until you find a good rhythm.

Try to involve your older kids with age-appropriate tasks that they can do to help mom and dad and help with the twins. This can be everything from doing household chores, helping with dinner, or helping with the laundry to actual hands-on care for the twins, like changing diapers and playing with them or feeding them. Depending on the age of your other children there should be something that they can do to help contribute and help care for the twins. It may not be fast, it may not be efficient, and it may not be how you would do it, but nevertheless your other children are eager to help and contribute and it gives them something that they can do to keep them busy in a productive way.

When my wife was on bed rest during our twin pregnancy, we hired a neighborhood teenager who came over and played with our other boys in the afternoon so my wife could rest. The same tactic can apply after the twins arrive. Consider recruiting a babysitter, a family member, or a friend to come over for an hour or two to help during the crazy part of the day. During the summer months, it is typically easier to recruit teenage kids to help since they are available during the day. In this way, your older kids will still get help and attention while your personal time, attention, and energy are limited.

Keep Siblings Busy While You Tend to the Twins

During the day, you'll have a similar challenge: how do you keep the other kids busy while you feed and tend to the twins?

Talk to other parents and see if you can swap kids. They take your kids one day and you take theirs the next. If your older kids can play independently with friends, having the extra kids in the house may not be a big deal. In fact, if they are so busy playing, it will seem easier than when you just have your kids running around.

Kids are always distracted by something new. This is a trick we use when we travel on long trips. Pull out a new toy, book, or activity that the kids haven't seen or haven't done in a while. Keep a bag of special items that you pull out periodically. This will likely keep their attention for at least a few minutes while you tend to the twins.

If your young children can physically help with caring for the twins, let them help! Our oldest son was three years old when our twin daughters were born. He loved to help by bringing us burp clothes or diapers or picking things up so we didn't have to bend down with a babe in arms. Take advantage of the selfless desires and love your older siblings have for their newborn twin siblings.

Before you need your kids' help, make sure that you teach and show them how to do the job you need before the actual need arises. This way they are prepared and ready to help when the moment arises.

Our kids are always the most quiet and still when they are eating. Keep a supply of healthy snacks available to distract your kiddos when you have to take care of the twins.

Try some of these options and you'll buy yourself a least a few moments to tend to a fussy baby, change a diaper, or feed your newborn twins.

Older Children's Activities

If you've got older kids with activities outside the home (like soccer, dance, etc.), you'll need to reset expectations on what is possible with them and infant twins.

You need to communicate to your older children that these babies are going to require a lot of work. You as a parent will be involved with the twins and their care. This means that the older children might not be able to have and do everything they had before, at least temporarily. Maybe this means suspending an activity, or that a family friend will take them to their class for a while instead of you.

Your other kids are going to be jealous that they're losing the time and attention that they used to have. If you can promise a light at the end of the tunnel to help make this transition easier for them, that will help.

If you want to maintain the schedule you have with your other kids, especially if they have a lot of activities, you're likely going to have to just take the twins with you. We took our double stroller with our twins to lots of places — lots of places we didn't even think were possible, like on hiking trails and aquatic locations. There were many occasions where I split up duties with my wife. I would take some kids in a certain direction, and she would take the rest in another direction. Or I would stay home with the twins while she took the boys where they needed to be.

A word of caution: don't try to get pulled in too many directions. Simplify your life and activities until your twins are a bit older. Raising infant twins is hard enough without having to be in many different places at the same time.

CHAPTER TWELVE

Potty

Newborns average about 10 diapers a day per baby. So your newborn twins will need about 10 diapers X 30 days X 2 babies = at least 600 diapers for the first month.

After about a month, diaper consumption goes down to about 8 diapers per day. You'll need eight diapers X 30 days X 2 babies = at least 480 diapers per month for a few more months.

After three to six months, your babies should fall into a regular pattern with more predictable diaper usage. The blow outs and leaks of the newborn days are gone and you'll see a pattern emerging. From three months to one year your twins should be down to about four to six diapers per day per child.

Based on averages (your twins' usage will vary) you are looking at using about 2,000 diapers by the time your twins turn six months old. That total tops 4000 diapers by their first birthday.

After the year mark, diaper use is usually down to about four a day: one change when they wake up, one before naps, one before bed, and one for the random poop that happens every day at unpredictable times. Your toddler twins will need 4 diapers X 30 days X 2 toddlers = 240 diapers per month.

This means your twins could use close to 3,000 diapers in the year between ages one and two. (Makes you want to potty train early, doesn't it?)

"Didn't we just buy a box of diapers?" you'll ask, surprised, when you see your stock running low. (The answer is always "yes," by the way.)

Once your twins potty train, you'll be free from the traditional diapers. However, in some cases, you might need Pull-ups for nap times and overnight sleeping until they master the overnight dryness too.

Unfortunately, Pull-ups (and especially the overnight extra absorbent kind) tend to be more expensive than regular diapers. Fortunately, the volume of diapers during this transition period is cut in half.

The reality of so many diapers is that you feel like you are always changing them. You are. You'll feel like you've got stacks of diapers all over the house. You do. It seems like your garbage is full of diapers. It is.

FROM YOUR FELLOW PARENTS OF TWINS…

"My daughter is the first girl to be born in my family in 60 years. Although I have changed the nappies of cousins and nephews, and been aware of their ability to spray when being changed, I was not aware a little girl can squirt just as well. Only took one face full of wee to dispel that myth!"

- Daniel Liam Ransom

Diaper Genies for Twins

We had one Diaper Genie for our twins, and it served us very well. This innovative device is a glorified trash can where you insert a dirty diaper, close the lid, twist the device, and the diaper is wrapped in a smell-containing plastic pouch.

Even though your twins go through a lot of diapers, you still only need one Diaper Genie for your twins. One pail will fill up quickly - especially in those early days when you're going through 10 diapers per newborn per day.

What the Diaper Genie does very well is to keep the smells contained. If you just have an open trash can in the bedroom or wherever you're changing your baby's diapers, it starts to smell pretty quickly and pretty bad. You don't have to keep taking the garbage out after every diaper. You can wait until it's full and then take that out to the trash.

You'll need to buy trash bag refills for the Diaper Genie, and those costs can add up. Don't buy two Diaper Genies. One of them is going to be enough for you, and you can use the extra money that you would've spent to purchase refills instead.

When to Move to the Next Size Diapers

Each size diaper corresponds to a weight range to help you know what size to buy for your babies. What you may not realize is that there is about a two-pound overlap between sizes. You don't necessarily need to max out the weight range on one size before moving up to the next size.

How do you know when the time is right? The solution is simple.

When your twins start having blowouts and leaks on a frequent basis, it is time to move up to the next diaper size. This may seem obvious, but in practice, it is not.

Your twins will have a poop that overflows the diaper and you'll be so busy cleaning it up that you won't see the pattern that is emerging.

If you hear yourself saying any of these things, it may be time to change diaper sizes:

- "Again! She had a blowout yesterday…"
- "What? Another blowout?"
- "Why does she keep overflowing her diaper?"
- "I really hate cleaning out these poopy clothes!"

Once you start to see multiple blowouts and on a recurring basis, go ahead and buy the next size diapers.

One of our girls seemed to be having the blowout problem more than her sister. So we moved up a size on one girl and not the other.

You may ask, "but what if we move up a size and the diapers are too big?" Don't let the "too big" possibility stop you from proceeding. Even if they don't fit today, your twins will keep growing and they can start wearing them in the near future.

I will say, that with our four kids, we've never had the problem of poop leaving a "too big" diaper.

Cloth Diapers vs. Disposable

If you don't want to go with disposable diapers, you can always use cloth diapers. Cloth diapers will cost you a couple hundred dollars to get all the diapers in the beginning. But after that, it's a lot cheaper, over time, compared to disposable diapers.

You will have to do more work with cloth diapers. You'll need to clean and wash them yourself in order to keep up with the twins. That means that you'll need to bring your A-game to the laundry arena, because if you get behind on laundry … no clean diapers.

Weigh the decision: do you want the convenience of disposable diapers or the cost effective and more environmentally friendly cloth diapers? There are certainly pros and cons to both routes.

There are cloth diaper services that will keep you stocked with all the diapers you need for a monthly fee. The costs for these types of services vary but in our city they run about $120/month for the amount of diapers that twins use. These types of services would save you the effort of cleaning all the diapers, but it does come with additional cost.

How do you pay for all of those twin diapers?

There are several options that you have to help reduce the cost of all your twins' diapers.

One of the services out there that many parents of twins use is called Amazon Mom. This is a subscription service where you sign up to receive regular shipments of diapers from Amazon.com. When you're enrolled in that program, you get a discount on the price compared to buying a package one at a time.

If you want to buy in bulk, you can also go to your local warehouse club store, like Costco or Sam's Club. We have a Costco membership, and we would use Costco diapers with our twins. Whenever we'd go to Costco, we'd stock up with big boxes to take care of our babies.

Additionally, stores like Target have store-brand diapers that compare, price-wise, favorably with national brands. I've also heard of some parents of twins going to a Target to purchase because they'll get the Target credit card, where you can get a percentage back on your purchases in the store, and so that makes the diapers even that much cheaper.

Ultimately, you want to be able to get your twins potty-trained as fast as possible and get them out of diapers, but you're probably going to be buying diapers for at least two to three years.

When to Potty Train Twins

When is the right time to potty train your twins? You may hear a lot about readiness and how to determine if your child is ready, but I'll save you some time: blow past all of that fluff. It really doesn't matter so much if your twins are ready as much as it matters that you and your wife are ready.

However, once you feel like you are ready to tackle this newest twin challenge, there are several other factors that will help you decide when you should potty train your twins.

Your Twins Want To Potty Train

We were reluctant to potty train our twin girls because we knew it would be a lot of work. This procrastination gave our girls time to mature. Slowly, over time, our girls started showing interest in using the potty like mommy and daddy. We found ourselves frequently taking them to the potty at their request.

If you wait long enough, your twins may very well ask to potty train.

You are Sick of Diapers

One of the challenges you have is the massive amount of diapers that twins use. This is a significant financial burden in addition to the hassle of changing all those diapers.

You will reach the point where you don't want to keep spending that money or dealing with packing diapers wherever you go. This may be a good time to start potty training.

You Aren't Going Anywhere

Potty training your twins is not an instantly completed task. Plan to train your twins when you won't be traveling for vacation or business. By sticking around the house you will have more control over accident cleanups and have the benefit of your home's familiarity.

Your Twins Can Communicate

Your twins' ability to communicate to you is a critical aspect of potty training. They don't necessarily need to be talking yet. Perhaps they are using baby signs to communicate. Regardless of the method, be sure you can understand your twins' needs and they understand your instructions. If they have demonstrated the ability to follow directions, that will help.

You Have One-on-One Time

We found it very helpful to potty train our girls one at a time. To teach them the mechanics of using the potty, I took all the other kids out of the house for a morning while my wife trained one daughter. The absence of sibling distractions and the constant parental attention helped each daughter focus on the task at hand.

You are Prepared

My wife and I love the book "Toilet Training in Less Than A Day" by Nathan Azrin and Richard Foxx. We used its positive reinforcement methods to teach each of our kids. Yes, you can teach your kid the logistics of using the potty in one day. Will they magically keep their pants dry immediately thereafter? No. Mastering their bodies will likely take a little longer.

Supplies You'll Need to Potty Train Twins

Before you begin potty training your twins, you need a plan. Ideally, this plan will cover what you will do and say, and how you will respond, react, encourage, support, cleanup, practice, help, and teach your twins.

We took the steps from the "Toilet Training in Less Than a Day" book and printed them out on papers that we hung up in the house the day we were training each of our twins. This helped us remember what we should do in the chaos of the moment.

For the Bathroom

While it is true that twins don't always need two of everything, the exception occurs with potty training. We found that when one of our twins wanted to go potty, the other almost always followed with a "Me, too!" When you are training your twins, you want to enable them to form good habits so you'll need to make provisions for them to both go potty at the same time.

You may think that if you have two bathrooms in your house that you are set. However, this isn't the case. In the early days of potty training, your twins will likely need help. If you are home alone, you can't realistically send one twin off to another bathroom while you stay with her sibling.

Be prepared for both twins needing to use the potty at one time.

You need to prepare one bathroom as the potty training bathroom. This should have a little potty training toilet, likely a hard plastic toy-looking one with a removable bowl. We used a Fisher-Price potty but turned off the sound and removed the batteries to avoid annoying sound effects.

Additionally, you'll want to acquire a child's toilet seat adapter that will fit on your full size toilet. Something like a padded seat with handles works great. They are relatively inexpensive and worth their weight in gold. This basic adapter keeps your child from falling into the toilet backside first.

You will also need step stools to help your twins step up to the big potty and to reach the sink for washing their hands. Make sure you have two stools if your bathroom can accommodate two; otherwise, look for a single stool that is wide enough for two children to stand on simultaneously.

Clothing

Loose fitting clothes are best for potty training your twins. You don't want them to have trouble pulling down their pants at the critical moment. Elastic waistbands are usually easiest for kids to pull up and down.

On training days, you may want to skip outerwear altogether and let your child spend the day in their undies. Buy underpants a size or two bigger than your child so they can pull them down quickly. Make sure you have plenty of clean replacements on hand and be prepared to do laundry every day to handle accidents.

Clean-Up Supplies

You will need to clean up four things: the twins, the bathroom, the floor (wherever accidents happen) and clothing.

Wet wipes are your best friend for cleaning up your twins, especially when they poop in their pants. Toilet paper is fine for general use, but sometimes you just need the extra 'umph' a wet wipe provides to clean a bum. You can use the wipes to clean out the underwear, too.

Get some disinfectant cleaner wipes for cleaning the hard surfaces in your bathroom during potty training: floor, sink, toilet, tub, etc. This enables you to disinfect with a quick swipe. You often won't have time for deep cleaning during potty training.

Have a supply of floor or carpet cleaner for handling accidents that will occur around your home. Hopefully you aren't too emotionally attached to your carpet, because it will take a beating while your twins learn to master the art of potty training.

Stock an adequate supply of laundry detergent and stain remover spray for the extra laundry you will be doing.

You will have poop accidents where your twins' underwear is so nasty you honestly don't know what to do. Don't worry, that is natural. It is especially hard to handle poop in public when you are away from your cleaning resources. In times like that, it is OK to let it go. Wrap those soiled undies up, drop them in the trash, and move on with your life.

Patience

The most essential supply you need to stock for happy and successful potty training is patience. You must remain calm and positive in your encouragement or things will quickly spiral out of control. Take your time, breathe deeply, and lower your expectations and things will work themselves out. Your twins will master using the potty.

You can download a list of supplies and gear you'll need to potty train your twins at www.dadsguidetotwins.com/more.

How to Potty Train Twins

The time has come to potty train your twins. You've got your stash of supplies and are ready to go. Let the games begin.

Potty training your twins really comes in two phases: teaching the skills and daily practice.

Decide Which Parent Will Train

Which parent should potty train the twins? You need to decide based on what makes the most sense in your situation. My wife and I took turns with each of our boys (singletons) and we decided that she would potty train our twins.

This step is all about expectations. Even though one of you will do the official training, the other spouse will need to support the trainer and reinforce the right behaviors for the trainees as well.

One At A Time

Feeling overwhelmed at the thought of training both twins at the same time? Take heart: it is fine to train each twin one at a time.

You Have to Teach Them

Your twins will not naturally know how to use the potty. They won't know how to pull down their pants, sit on the toilet, use the toilet paper, pull their pants up, and wash their hands unless you show them. These very tactical skills are essential to potty training and too often parents assume that kids just know how to do it. Your kids will absorb a certain amount of this routine from watching you, and as you approach training time, you can certainly give your toddler a play-by-play of what you are doing. But these skills won't be second nature to them. You need to set aside a day to teach and practice these basic skills.

Pick The Day

Look at your calendar and set aside "potty training day" for one of your twins. Mark it on the calendar and start talking to your child about that day. Get them excited about potty training by taking them to the store to pick out "big kid underpants" and help them prepare for the big day.

Potty Training Day needs to be a day when you are free from distractions and other obligations. You need to dedicate all your attention to the process and focus 100% on your child on this day.

Learning the Skills

As I've mentioned before, the book "Toilet Training in Less Than A Day" has fabulous step-by-step instructions on how to train your child.

It starts with your child "training" a doll that can wet herself. Your child will help the doll to learn how to use the potty. In so doing, your child will learn the steps herself.

After the doll exercise, you will need to have your child drink lots of fluids throughout the day. The book's method uses positive reinforcement so you reward the child at regular intervals through the day whenever she has dry pants.

Accidents are followed up with practice drills reinforcing how to run to and get on the potty.

By the end of the day, your child can physically use the toilet by herself. Truly amazing.

Continual Reinforcement

After the mechanics of potty use are mastered, you will need to constantly praise and reinforce your twins during the subsequent weeks and months for keeping their pants dry. Over time they will become more self-sufficient but be sure to stick around and support them until they can go unprompted and unassisted.

Positive Peer Pressure

One of our girls wanted to potty train and the other parked her heels and refused. She said, "No. Diapers," upon peeing her pants once. So we trained one and left the other in diapers.

However, as the diaper-laden girl saw all the attention and praise her sister was getting, she quickly wanted to train, too. Leverage that peer pressure to influence the other, but balance that with respecting your child's desires to train.

CHAPTER THIRTEEN

Travel

How Soon Can We Travel With the Twins?

If you've got healthy, full-term twins, you should be able to travel even when your kids are newborns. How you travel may impact your plans. We traveled with our girls for day trips by car when they were still infants and by plane when they were just shy of one year old.

Travel with twins is much different than any travel you've done previously. When you travel with twins you'll have to reset your expectations of when you can travel, where you can go, and what you will be able to do. The travel habits and patterns you've gotten into before twins are not going to stay the same.

You'll need to plan your trips and daily activities around your twins' nap and feeding times. You have to consider sleeping arrangements for hotels or rentals that you're going to get. You'll need to apply airline rules to your personal scenario. All of these different logistics impact traveling with your twins.

Please give your newborn twins time to adjust to life in the cruel, germ-filled world. While a baby's immune system is good and getting better, try to give your babies more time to get established and strong before venturing out on a big trip. If your trip isn't absolutely necessary, postpone it for later.

You'll be taking your twins to the doctor a lot over the first few months for well-baby checkups. Make sure your travel plans don't interfere with getting your twins to the pediatrician.

The younger your twins, the less likely you've figured out what you're doing. You're still learning how to manage and feed twins. Once your twins are on a predictable feeding and sleeping schedule, you can plan your trip to take best advantage of those times.

Before you venture out on a cross-country trip, try getting out of the house with the twins first. You may want to experiment to see how well your babies travel by doing short trips at first. With that success under your belt, you can then stretch out to longer, more complicated adventures. If you're having trouble with a trip to the store or a walk around the block, you probably want to wait before you go out of town on a big trip.

Air travel with infants is generally very safe. However, some airlines will let you fly your babies only when they are older than two weeks old. You'll need to have a copy of the birth certificates. If you're flying before the twins turn two weeks old, you'll need a medical release note from the pediatrician. Check with your specific airline to confirm the details of traveling with newborns.

In retrospect, our infant twins were easier to travel with than our under-age-two toddler twins. Infants sleep or stay put in your arms. Toddlers (especially as lap children) are a constant tornado of motion and energy. Unfortunately, controlling twinadoes on an airplane is not easy. More on that in a bit.

You'll find that each trip with your twins is different. They mature a little bit between trips and every time has different challenges. The logistical challenges change over time based on the age of your children and your chosen mode of transportation.

What to Pack When Traveling with Twins

Traveling with twins is a challenge but it doesn't have to be impossible. A successful trip with your twins begins with good planning. It will be more fun for mom and dad as long as a lot of thought goes into preparing for your trip.

The best thing to do is make a list of all items you wish to bring along, including any snacks, toys, clothing, diapers and toiletries. Your packing list will vary based on your twins' age but every twin (regardless of age) will need provisions for food, water, potty, clothing, and entertainment.

When traveling with twins, you will need to be sure you have items for them such as:

- Formula, bottles, nipples, and bottle warmer, jars of food and spoons
- Diapers, rash ointments and baby wipes
- Baby or child toiletries such as shampoos, baby wash, cloths, combs, toothbrushes, etc.
- Snacks such as teething biscuits or cookies, raisins, breadsticks, fruit bars, juice boxes, finger sandwiches, rice cakes, cut up grapes, snack packs of fruit, applesauce pouches, etc.
- Pacifiers, food dishes, food utensils, and wipes or damp cloth in a plastic bag for sticky fingers and faces
- An outfit for each day away, along with a couple of extras for those unavoidable accidents
- An extra shirt for each parent, easily accessible during travel in the case of spit ups or blowout diapers
- Toys, some old and some new, for a variety to avoid boredom and captivate by the "new" factor
- Sunscreen, hats, rash suits, baby-safe bug spray
- Double Umbrella stroller – easier to travel with unless your twins are too young to sit in them
- A camera and/or video camera and extra film or memory cards
- Tylenol, Benadryl or any other medication your twins may need on, during, or after the trip
- Pack 'n Play, car seats, booster seats

As you can see from the list above, it is really easy to over pack with twins. Make your list and then make note of the things you can purchase once you arrive at your destination. If you'll have time to do laundry on your trip, pack half the clothes.

How to Survive Air Travel with Twins

Air travel is difficult and costly because of the rising costs of both tickets and extra fees like baggage charges. If your twins are under age two, they can ride on your lap for free. However, if you pay for them to have their own seats, it is nice to have them buckled into their car seats so they don't run all over the plane.

When traveling by plane with twins, you will want to pack lightly and focus primarily on your children's needs. Sorry, you probably won't be able to relax much on the plane! Make a list of all necessities for the trip and stick to your list. Just the necessities alone for yourselves and the twins will be enough luggage to haul on a plane, because it's not just the luggage you'll be hauling. Given the fact that your twins will most likely need a car seat in order to get to and from the airport, picture what it will look like with luggage, 2 car seats, and a stroller.

We took a family vacation in the month before our girls turned two years old. While it was cheaper on our pocketbook, it definitely wore my wife and me out. Our biggest challenge was keeping the girls still and on our laps during takeoff, landing, and other "keep your seatbelt on" moments.

In fact, on a family trip we had made six months earlier, I promised myself that I would rather pay for them to have their own seats on the next trip than travel with them as lap children. However, when it came down to price we opted for the cheaper (free) fare and simply dealt with the mayhem in flight.

You should have a good idea of your twins' behavior in confined spaces (think long car trips or stuck in a shopping cart) and can weigh their expected behavior with the price of the extra tickets.

While flying with free lap children is cheaper, the most secure location for anyone on a plane is fully strapped into their seats. This includes infants. The challenge with many parents of infant twins is affording two additional seats on the plane. Most domestic US flights are at least $300-$400 round trip. The trade-off between saving money and safety is one that each parent must seriously consider before boarding the plane.

Here are some tips for surviving an airplane flight with twins in tow:

- Flying earlier in the day means that everyone is fresher and it's more likely the twins will be at their best compared to later in the day. The downside to this is that flights are more likely to be full earlier in the day. Something to consider based on the needs of your family: full flight and better behaved, or extra space and worn-out kiddos?
- Make sure that your car seats are airplane-approved. You can look for that on the label on the side of the car seat to see if they are approved for airplane use.
- Get in the pre-boarding group to give you plenty of time to get the babies strapped into their car seats and settled, or let them climb all over you and push all the buttons before the rest of the passengers board.
- For planning purposes, it's good to know that you can only have one lap child per row on the plane. This is because there is only one extra oxygen mask for any row of seats.
- Divide and conquer children and responsibilities with your spouse before you board the plane.
- Get a direct flight to your destination. Anyone traveling with kids will tell you it's easier to get on a plane and get off a plane one time than it is to change or connect with other flights. Basically, you want to reduce the amount of time you are on the plane with your kids. It will even be worth the extra money if you can avoid changing planes en route.
- Check all the luggage you can. Especially if you have other kids, you won't have any free hands for extra luggage to carry on. Take your kids, supplies for them, and a lot of patience. Check everything else.
- You can check your car seats. Many airlines have large plastic bags that you can put your seats in to protect them from dirt during transit.

- Take your double stroller and check it at the gate right before you get on the plane. You don't want to have to carry your twins and carry-on bags through the airport terminals. Let the stroller carry the baby burden and maybe you can even sling some bags on the back of it.
- Read the labels of the airplane snacks before you give them to your babies. You don't want to be introducing new foods or risk allergic reactions when confined on a plane.
- Your twins will want to play with the peanut snacks because of the texture and sound of the packaging. While this will provide needed diversion for at least ten minutes, if your twins have teeth, realize that it is possible for them to chew a hole in the packaging and make a really big mess (my wife learned the hard way on this one).
- Have a sequence of toys and activities you can pull out over time during the flight to entertain your twins. Attention spans are short, so plan accordingly.
- Make sure your twins have something to eat, drink, or suck on during takeoff and landing. This will help alleviate any pressure in their ears and will prevent extended pain-induced crying fits. We like using (and the kids always love) candy suckers.

If you have other kids and have traveled with them before, you probably know a lot of these tips already. However, with twins you've got twice as many things to worry about.

The bonus of twins is that they are such an anomaly that people in the airport, on the plane, and during your trip will not only stop and comment, "Oh! Twins!" but will be more likely to help you when they see your hands are full. Take advantage of those that offer to help.

FROM YOUR FELLOW PARENTS OF TWINS…

"Since both of our families live far away, our girls (now one year old) are rather seasoned travelers. They do quite well on flights, and have had very few fussy airplane moments. Other passengers, however, are sometimes quick to react when they see a baby board — and their disdain is clear. When the girls were six months old, I got on a flight first with daughter number one. A woman already seated in the front row said - with clear dissatisfaction - 'Oh. A baby.' With a broad smile, just as my husband and baby number two (in an outfit identical to her sister's) boarded, I said - 'And it's your lucky day! There are TWO of them!'"

- Heather Kurut

Flying with Twins: Best Seating Arrangements

Once your twins turn two years old, flying as lap children is no longer an option. You need to think strategically about how you want to make seating arrangements.

When you look at flying with twins and getting seats on an airplane, there are a couple of scenarios.

Option 1: have an adult and a twin on each side of the aisle (assuming the airplane has at least two seats on each side of the aisle).

Option 2: have three people on one side of the aisle, and another parent on the other side of the aisle. For example, you have mom and the twins on one side, and dad on the other side of the aisle.

Option 3: get two rows of seats, one behind the other, where you have a parent and a twin on one row, and then, the row right behind them, you have another parent and a twin.

Keep in mind that if your twins are in car seats, they both need to be in a window seat. This is so the car seats don't block the aisle and exit in case of emergencies.

When we traveled with our toddler girls and paid for their tickets, we loved having them in their car seats. It was a huge hassle to carry the car seat through the terminal, get it on a plane, and install it on the plane with the seat belt. But once the seats were in place and our girls buckled in, it was a big help because it kept the girls in their seats.

You know that the seat belts on an airplane are very easy to open, especially for kids. They just flip the little latch and they're out. Your kids will want to move around, jump around, and run around on the airplane. Having them buckled into their car seats prevents a lot of mischief, especially when the seat belt sign is on and the captain has asked that you stay seated. Kids are generally accustomed to being in their car seats during car travel, so buckling them in on a plane won't phase them much.

Whichever seating arrangement you choose, make sure that each parent can be self-sufficient in taking care of their twin traveling companion. Assume that the other parent is going to be out of reach or have their hands full. Whoever is with a twin needs to have a backpack full of supplies to take care of that twin by him or herself. You can always switch parent-twin combinations, maybe when you change planes or on the return trip.

I recommend each parent with a twin sit on each side of the aisle. And if your twin is not in a car seat, have the twin sit in the middle seat and you, as the parent, on the aisle so you can reach across the aisle and talk to your spouse or pass baby supplies back and forth.

Flying Alone With Twins

If you do have to travel alone with two babies, there are some things to keep in mind to make the trip a little bit easier for you. When you're flying, the general rule is one child per lap. So regardless of whether your twins can fly free, you're still going to need to pay for at least two tickets, one for you and one for a twin. If you have it in your budget, you may want to get three tickets - one for each of your twins and one seat for you. This gives you the option to have your twins in their own seats, and they can be resting or entertained next to you. Then your hands are free to help soothe and pick one up to cuddle or to feed them, or whatever you need to do.

If it's not in your budget for the third ticket, consider getting a car seat carrier that you can strap on your back like a backpack. You'll probably look like a pack mule walking through the airport, but you'll be grateful to have the car seat to contain one of the twins.

Because you are alone and because you have twins, you're going to have a lot of sympathetic people around you, especially the flight crew. The flight attendants are going to be more willing to offer you help and make sure that you're comfortable. Make sure you're over the top in showing your appreciation to them and giving them thanks for the things that they're doing for you.

That also means that you can't take advantage of the flight attendants. You need to do your part to help keep your babies soothed, cool, calm, and collected. Remember to take plenty of supplies to help with your twins. Have a stock of formula if you're bottle-feeding or food if they're already on solid foods. Bring toys and entertainment, including books, which can keep your twins entertained and busy.

How to Keep Toddler Twins Occupied on Road Trips

Taking your toddler twins on a road trip requires some planning and patience. Road trips with toddler twins are all about maximizing their attention span. Instead of a few activities or distractions that could occupy lots of time, think about lots of activities that have short durations.

Try your twins in different seats to make the trip more interesting.

Try shuffling car seats around during your trip. Perhaps this can be done every day you are driving or whenever you stop for a meal. We found that when the kids had a new environment in the vehicle, it helped keep them happy. The bonus was that when the kids argued over who got to sit where, we could appease them with the promise of moving seats later.

Your toddler twins probably already have tons of toys. The toys that will best serve you on a road trip are new ones. New toys seem to grab your kids' attention more easily than one they have been playing with the last several weeks. That being said, if your twins are attached to a favorite toy or stuffed animal, don't force them to give it up in favor of something new.

Try digging up some old toys they haven't seen in awhile. Alternatively, go to the dollar store and pick up some cheap new toys that would be easy to play with in the car. Don't give all the toys to the kids up front. Pull them out strategically during the road trip so you can maximize their distracting power.

As with toys, bring books your kids either love or haven't yet discovered. Visit your local library and load up on books that you can take on your trip. If your kids don't independently look at books of their own volition or if you get carsick sitting backwards and reading to the little ones, try read-along CDs. You remember those, right? The ones with the chime when it's time to turn the page? They can be found at just about any bookstore or library.

Have favorite songs that your toddler twins like to listen to in the car around town? Time to make a Road Trip Playlist. The scenery will pass more quickly if the kiddos have a groovy tune or two to sing along with. Add a few of mom and dad's favorites and introduce the kids to songs you like while you have a captive audience. Let loose and be even a little silly, and you'll make some good memories with your kids.

Toddler twins might be too young to enjoy traditional road trip games like Road Trip Bingo or the ABC game where you look for letters on signs and cars. Nevertheless, they can probably look for trains, cactus, windmills or other obvious features that you can turn into an 'I Spy' game.

Pack some healthy snacks that you can pull out at the opportune moment during the trip. You don't want to have to stop every time the kids are hungry. Load up a cooler or bag with food to help you get further down the road before you have to stop. Food is always a good bribe for good behavior as well.

Traditionally, mom and dad ride up front in the car. On road trips, try putting one parent in the back with the kids. This will work more easily if you have a mini-van or SUV. The kids are distracted because "Hey, mommy is sitting by me." The parent can then play with the kids or read stories to them. Be sure both mom and dad take turns rotating with the kids to help maintain parental sanity.

When all else fails, you can use movies. Get a portable DVD player or iPod or whatever you have and let your kids watch movies. On our first big 54-hour road trip, we managed to go all but the last six hours before we needed to pull out the movies. We simply kept our toddler twins (and their older brothers) occupied with the aforementioned activities.

Frequent stops may be needed when traveling by car. Your twins (like most kids) will always need to go potty a few miles down the road after you just stopped. Our family travel rule is that when we stop to go potty, everyone goes potty. No exceptions.

It won't take long before your kids realize that there's a difference between driving to the grocery store and spending a significant amount of time in the car on a road trip. It's okay to let them get a little bored. It's okay for you to not be thrusting the next activity in front of their faces as soon as the current one is over. You'll smile as you see them get creative with entertaining themselves.

Should You Use Leashes for Twins?

Once your twins get mobile, they will be off to the races. It is hard to contain toddler twins, especially when they run in opposite directions. This can be a safety concern, especially when out in public. You don't want to lose them or have them run off and get into danger. Because of these realities, you may consider getting leashes for your twins.

When you put your twins in leashes and go out in public, you'll get reactions from other people. You'll notice weird looks or even scoffs and laughs. You're the one with the twins and your hands are full. If the leashes are keeping your twins safe, you shouldn't care what others think.

One thing to note is that the twins always seem to run in opposite directions. If you are holding one leash in each hand, your arms will feel like they are getting pulled out of their sockets. So hang on tight!

If you solely rely on the leashes to keep your twins in line, you'll fail miserably. You must constantly be teaching and setting expectations with your twins. Use the leashes as a safety net to keep them from wandering too far, but remember: twins aren't dogs. Teach them to hold your hand and walk by your side. Explain why they should stay near you and praise them when they do.

We found the leashes extremely helpful with our twins when we'd make big trips or go on vacation. Of all the things to worry about on a trip, you don't want to worry about your twins running off.

However, if you wait until your trip to try out your leashes, your twins may revolt. Try them on and use them around the house or at the grocery store. This way, they will be able to adjust and be used to the leashes on your big trip.

Eventually your twins will outgrow their leashes. Either they will be old enough to hold your hand and stay put, or they will constantly be unbuckling their own harnesses.

Our twins did well with leashes that looked more like a backpack or teddy bear than a dog leash. Our girls loved the stuffed animal backpack leashes and wore them for fun around the house. The extra bonus of a backpack leash is that you can stash kids' toys or a sippy cup in there and not have to carry it yourself.

You'll find a list of top-rated leashes you could use for your twins at www.dadsguidetotwins.com/more.

How to Survive an Amusement Park with Twins

Although I had sworn to never take my kids to Disneyland until everyone was potty trained and they were all tall enough to ride all the rides, we somehow found our family at Disneyland with our four kids, ages four and under. On our first trip to Disneyland, our twins were 10 months old. We also later survived trips to Sea World and Six Flags with our little kids in tow. We had a blast and you can, too.

Discussing princess etiquette with Snow White

Some amusement parks are more kid-friendly than others. Take time before you arrive at the park to spec out things like restrooms (particularly family-style ones), mother's nursing lounges, stroller parking areas, and if there are any courtesy refrigerators where you can store food or milk. Most parks have maps online that you can study and map out your strategy. A little bit of prior planning will help the day go so much smoother. You don't want to spend the day sitting on a bench with your crying twins, wondering why you came in the first place.

At Disneyland, we were surprised by how many rides didn't have a height requirement. We were able to wait in line together as a family and ride the rides together as a family, even with our baby girls in tow. Be aware that even if height requirements are met, some rides need an adult to ride with the child until they are at least 7 years old.

You don't want to carry your twins in your arms all day long. We saw plenty of tired parents who did just that. Be prepared: take your double twin stroller. Aside from the obvious purpose of a stroller, the stroller also acts as a pack mule for carrying bags and souvenirs that will easily fit over the handles. Just be aware that your heavy bags are counterbalanced by the babies in the seats. So when you take the babies out, expect the stroller to fall backwards if it is indeed that pack mule just mentioned.

The stroller will also double as the sleeping quarters about halfway through the day. Since your infant twins are used to taking naps, they will eventually get so tired that they will just fall asleep in the stroller.

In addition to our stroller, we took two Baby Bjorn front baby carriers when our girls were infants. These turn you and your wife into pseudo-kangaroos with your babies strapped firmly to your chest. These carriers were invaluable in being able to hold our twins without sacrificing the use of our arms while we waited in line (which we needed for their two brothers). We even took our girls on several rides while still in their carriers. Plus, if you and your wife are walking or standing next to each other, you'll get lots of "Oh, look at the twins!" comments.

Before you get to the park, check that the amusement park you are attending will allow you to bring in food and water. Some are more accommodating than others. Your kids will be accustomed to certain foods and you need to have those on hand for consumption throughout the day. This is particularly important if your babies have started solids but aren't past the pureed food stage. If you aren't allowed to bring food in, make sure you have food in a cooler in the car. Leave the park for meals and have your own little tailgating party.

Most amusement park food is expensive. Try to buy fewer meals than you have number of kids and you'll likely be able to share across the family and still satisfy everyone. This will save you a few dollars with each meal you eat at the park.

Water is also key, especially since you don't want to pay exorbitant prices for water once you're in the park. Most parks will allow you to bring your own water with you. You will need water to keep you, your wife, and the kids hydrated, as well as needing it to mix with formula for bottles.

This may be stating the obvious, but make sure everyone gets a liberal covering of sunscreen throughout the day. Babies have more sensitive skin than adults, which is prone to burning faster. You don't want to have a fun day at the park only to be up all night with crying babies who can't move without their sunburn hurting them.

Your toddler twins will demonstrate their very distinct wishes about what rides to ride or not and what to do. On a subsequent trip to Disneyland, one of our girls loved seeing all the princesses and getting their autographs. Our other girl wanted to ride roller coasters like Big Thunder Mountain or Space Mountain repeatedly. Be prepared to split up the family if needed to attend to the wishes of each twin. For example, I took our roller coaster-loving daughter and our sons on a ride while my wife waited 90 minutes with the other daughter to see Rapunzel.

If your twins are too small to go on a ride but you don't want to miss it, fear not. Many amusement parks will let you do a kid or baby swap so each parent can go on a ride. This will let one parent brave the lines while the other distracts the kids or takes them to see something else. When the riding parent is done, the other can get on the ride (typically by entering through the exit).

On subsequent trips to Disneyland, we had several Disney cast members stop and measure both our girls even though they are identical and the same height! So don't get frustrated when you seem to repeat the same process over and over again with your twins. As your twins get bigger and start to reach height requirements, don't be surprised if you find yourself jumping through the hoops of park policies over and over.

Going to amusement parks with little kids isn't really for your entertainment. You will go on rides you won't normally ride. But you will find joy in watching your twins' reactions to everything going on around them instead of the thrill of the ride itself.

Camping With Twins

It is the middle of the night and you've finally fallen asleep despite the chilly air and the hard ground.

But then you are suddenly poked and prodded by a little child that needs to go to the potty.

You know the latrine is a good walk away and that your girls are scared of all the spider webs and bugs that live there. And yet, for a moment, you consider sending your little daughter out with a flashlight to take care of it herself.

Nevertheless, you wake up, get your shoes on and prepare to jump out of the tent.

But wait. Your other daughter sleeps peacefully, unaware that you are leaving.

Surely she will wake the moment after you leave and burst into tears when she finds herself alone.

Surely, she too will need to go potty.

So you wake her up, get her shoes on and trudge with both daughters to the latrine. You stand guard so the bugs won't bite.

With the deed done, you head back to the tent, take shoes off, and help the kiddos crawl back into their sleeping bags.

You rest for a little bit longer until you are once again wakened by a little voice telling you it is time for breakfast.

Camping is great! Especially with twins.

My twin girls were 4 years old when I took them camping by myself.

Well, it wasn't really by myself. We went with our church group on a Daddy-Daughter camp out.

The girls were so excited they couldn't contain themselves. While we had gone camping before as a family, this was the first time we were on our own.

As a father with very young girls, my mind was swirling with the possibilities of them standing on fire ant mounds, rolling around in poison ivy, or getting lost in the woods. Fortunately, the great outdoors were kind to us. Here are some lessons we learned that can help you when you go camping with your twins.

I'll be the first to admit that camping with my girls was fun. Twins seem to have a way of doing things together and discovering new things together that makes everything more exciting. Soak in the fun and take time to watch your twins and see how they interact with each other and their new environment while camping.

Because there are so many things to discover outside, you'll notice that one twin will get the other in trouble. "Hey, look at that…" from one sister often leads to the other taking the action the first was too afraid to do herself. It seems that the twins share bad ideas and accelerate the trouble they can find. These ideas, which seem great to them at the time, often lead to tears – but typically funny stories after the fact.

Make sure you pack double the gear. Our girls liked having their own backpacks (that they helped pack) with supplies and clothes. Double sleeping bags were also handy even though the girls only used up a fraction of the space inside one.

As a Boy Scout, I learned that you always need to have your buddy. The joy of twins is that you have a built-in buddy. Tell your twins that they are each other's buddy and need to stick together. They need to always be able to see each other. If one of them gets hurt, the other can help or seek out help.

Camping with twins is super fun. You'll have more adventures than you could have anticipated!

CHAPTER FOURTEEN

Memories

Enjoy the Quickly Passing Moments with Infant Twins

Newborn twins will wear you out and make you miserable — if you let them. However, the misery can be countered by the happy and joyful moments of watching your little twins.

If you don't pay attention to the joy of your little twins, you'll soon realize they have grown up and you didn't notice.

Here are some tips to help you to savor the early months with your twins.

Go into your twins' room and watch them sleep. I loved watching our girls when they were newborns and sleeping in the same crib. They always tended to lean into each other. As they started to move about, they often ended up in very random sleeping arrangements with parts of one twin on top of the other.

What quirks can you observe with your sleeping twins? How does that change as they get older?

Tummy time with any newborn is fun. Put two newborns on the floor and you get a real show. Each experiences the frustration of trying to lift her head off the floor but also interacts with the other twin. Tummy time with twins promises to never have a dull moment.

Pay close attention to how your twins interact with each other and with you during tummy time. Get down on the floor and encourage your newborns verbally. Do they respond in sync or are they each doing their own thing?

Nothing is cuter than smiling babies. You'll eventually reach the stage when your twins smile because they are happy instead of a bodily process or for some physical reaction.

Can you make your twins smile? Does the same thing make both smile, giggle, or laugh?

When breastfeeding didn't work with our twin girls, we successfully bottle fed them. This was a great opportunity for me as a dad to participate in the process. I loved holding one of my little girls and hearing the sounds of her rhythmically drinking her meal. It amazed me how they could seemingly be asleep and yet still down an entire bottle of formula. Other times it was a challenge to even get them awake enough to feed at all.

I loved playing with my babies' toes or fingers when feeding them.

What can you admire about your little one during feeding time? What eating habits do your twins have? What sounds do they make? What mannerisms make you smile?

Nothing makes you feel more like a father of twins than holding both at the same time. Newborn twins can easily be held in a double football hold. However, that won't last forever, so enjoy it while you can.

Once they have better control over their heads and necks, they will be a little easier to scoop up. Before you know it, they'll be standing in their cribs and holding their arms out to you, waiting for you to pick them up and have some fun.

From there, it's not too much longer before you can throw one on your back and have one hugging your front as you do a double piggyback ride to bed.

How many different ways can you hold your twins? Can you pick them both up by yourself?

Take a second look at the day-to-day interactions with your twins. See past the repetition and trials and focus on the special moments you can share with both of them. There is joy in this amazing journey just waiting to be seen.

How to Remember Your Twins' First Year

The nurse at our pediatrician's office is a mother of twins and gave us a great piece of advice to help us remember the first year of our twins' lives:

Set aside a day of the week to take a few minutes of video of your twins.

Why? Because the first year will pass like a blur and before you know it, you won't have any video or pictures of your babies.

Remember that you'll be sleep deprived for several months after the arrival of your twins. Putting a system in place will help compensate for your frazzled mental state.

If you take a little video every week, you'll have a fabulous time line of your twins' growth and development that you can showcase at their first birthday or save to embarrass them when they get married.

The Only Way to Get Pictures With Your Twins

One of my regrets about our twins' first year was that I didn't get more pictures with both of my girls.

You may have a similar problem. If you don't actively make the effort to get pictures with you and both of your twins, it just won't happen.

It may seem a little silly to plan for pictures, like it is a little contrived, forced, or posed. But if you don't plan for it, you won't get any pictures of you with your babies. Why? Numerous reasons:

- Perhaps you are the one that always takes the pictures. If you are behind the camera, you're not in the picture.
- If you've got other kids, they will be asking for attention, too, as soon as they see the camera.
- The bigger your twins get, the harder it is to physically pick both of them up at the same time for a picture.
- It is difficult to take a self-portrait by holding out the camera in one hand while holding a baby in the other since you've got two babies.

How do you make sure you get pictures of you and your twins?

Plan for it. Keep it always on the front of your mind.

I found it helpful to make a point of getting pictures with my twins on major events and holidays. For example, every holiday and birthday I try to get pictures with my twins. Do I always get pictures on these days? No. But if you don't try, then you'll never get them.

The hard pictures to get are of you and your twins in everyday settings. The trick here is to keep your camera or smartphone close at hand.

When you see your twins doing something cute, funny, or spectacular, don't just think, "Oh, that's awesome." Go get your camera (or ask your wife to grab the camera) and take a picture of you and the kiddos.

There are a lot of things about life that are fleeting. Documenting life with photos is a great way to preserve the memories.

Photo Tips for Twins

Hopefully you'll be taking pictures of your twins during your daily activities. However, it is nice to hire a photographer to take some pictures of your twins and family. When it is time to take more staged pictures, there are some photo tips for twins you can follow to make the experience better for everyone involved. Some tips apply at all ages; others will change as your twins grow up.

When taking photos of your twins, you'll want to remember that twins are individuals. Of course you may want a picture of the two of them, but consider having individual photos taken as well. This will help them develop their own identity.

It will be up to you to decide whether your twins will wear matching outfits in their photos. You could let them wear different clothes for their individual photos. Whatever you decide, there are a few guidelines that always apply. Brightly colored clothing or clothes with loud designs can distract from the main point of the photo — your twins' faces. If you are having a professional photo shoot, consider taking the twins' picture clothing with you to the shoot and changing them into it there. This reduces the chance of spills or accidents that could spoil the outfits.

Expect your twins to run in opposite directions at picture time.

In my experience, some children don't mind standing still or smiling on request, but others don't like being bossed around. Rather than shouting orders at the twins during their photo shoot, think of ways to make it fun for them. Ask them for pose ideas or have a game to see who can make the best smile. Sing a favorite song, and if they are preschool age or older, change a word or two as you sing. The look on their faces when they realized that you sang "London Bridge is falling up" or "Ring around the Rosie, teddy bears are cozy" will make for some priceless pictures. As your twins get older and begin to have a mind of their own, it may help to explain to them what will happen at the photo shoot so they can cooperate.

Whether you take your own photos of your twins or hire a photographer, schedule a time for the photo shoot that agrees with your twins' daily routine. Take photos when your twins are rested and fed, like after a nap and meal. Trying to shoot photos of twins later in the day when they are tired is asking for trouble.

It's hard enough to get one child to sit still for a nice photo, and the difficulty is compounded with twins. It may help to remember that, even if there are no perfect smiles, the photos that capture how your twins really are will make memories.

FROM YOUR FELLOW PARENTS OF TWINS…

"During newborn pictures we had to get at least one diaperless shot with our baby girl and baby boy. Nature called and our little boy started a runny mess of number two on the photographer's blanket. My wife and I were embarrassed and apologizing over and over while scrambling to clean it up. In the process, little girl's number two nature called and it sprayed all over little boy and the blanket. All we could do was bust out in hilarity. We got them all fixed up and managed to get that perfect picture."

- Dustin Marinucci

How to Tell Newborn Twins Apart in Pictures

With all the pictures you are taking of your newborn twins, how will you tell them apart?

When your twins arrive, they will be swaddled up by the nurses at the hospital and whisked away to the nursery to warm up and be measured.

Since the hospital has a standard set of blankets and head warmers, both of your twins will likely be swaddled in the same exact materials.

Yikes! Which twin is which?

Fortunately, as soon as they are born, each twin gets an ID tag (typically around the ankle or wrist) with "baby a" and "baby b" printed on it.

This is fine for identifying your babies in person. However, when you are looking at pictures you took of your newborn twins, you won't be able to see that ID tag.

Months later, you'll look back and try to figure out which baby is which.

A trick we used that turned out to be very helpful was to put a visual marker in the background of the picture to help identify the baby. This memory device will help you later.

I used a small yellow piece of paper placed somewhere in the picture with our "baby a". This way whenever we went back to look at pictures we instantly knew which twin was which.

Eventually, you can move on to using color-coded clothes or relying on distinctive physical characteristics to tell your twins apart in pictures. However, in those initial moments after the twins are born, have a backup plan. Put some memory device in the background of the picture that will help you for years to come.

How to Overcome the Foggy First Year with Twins

In battle, soldiers are often dazed or inhibited by the "fog of war." This fog comes from smoke, explosions, shell shock, lack of information, etc.

As a parent of twins, you have your own fog of war. This fog is thickest during your twins' first year.

Remember the last time you drove when there was a heavy fog? It was hard to see far ahead or behind your car. You had to drive slowly and were constantly on guard so you didn't run into anything.

You'll be in a similar fog with your new twins for several reasons:

- You'll be suffering from sleep deprivation.
- There will be no time to relax.
- You'll constantly be taking care of one baby or the other.
- Every day will seem like the one before.
- You won't be eating as well as you should since you're so busy with the babies.
- If you have other kids, they will be extra demanding of your attention because you, out of necessity, are giving more to the twins.
- If your twins were in the NICU, you'll have logged countless hours at the hospital.

This foggy haze will cloud your judgment and make days quite challenging.

You can make the first year easier for you and your family. Just be mindful of your body, situation, and family members:

- Plan ahead – as my mother-in-law always told my wife, "Plan for the worst, expect the best, and take what comes."
- Stock the freezer with easy ready-to-heat-up meals – for when you're hungry but don't have time to cook (which will happen a lot)
- Stick to a schedule – so both you and your twins have a sense of normalcy

- Sleep when your babies sleep – if you are tired, get some rest and let the "to-do" list wait for later
- Eat healthily – you'll need the energy to keep up with your twins
- Keep logs of vital tasks (feeding and diapering babies) – this will help supplement your fuzzy memory
- Get out of the house – and don't forget to take your wife with you
- Exercise as you can – take care of your body and it will help you with the demands of the first year
- Get a helper to relieve or assist you – an extra pair of hands will make life a lot easier
- Enjoy the happy moments – yes, there will be funny, memorable, and happy moments during the first year. Enjoy them!

Don't worry, it won't be foggy forever. Just like the sun burns away the morning fog, so shall time and constantly growing twins clear the fog for you.

Keep your chin up and hang in there!

Halloween Costume Ideas for Twins

It can be a challenge to come up with clever Halloween costume ideas for twins – whether your twins are the same gender or not. However, if you are open to a bit of creativity and hunting around to find the ideal costume, you can find some creative costumes for your twins.

One year our girls dressed up as Dorothy and the Wicked Witch from *Wizard of Oz*. This was a fun pairing, especially when they were standing together. Even if they were separated, the costumes still stood on their own and people could guess what they were.

The movie *Despicable Me* has spawned Minion costumes that are a natural match for twins (or any multiples). To make these costumes, all you need are two yellow hoodies, overalls and some goggles. Maybe a little yellow face paint to help finish the illusion off!

The superhero world is massive at the moment, with the Marvel films bringing comic book superheroes back to the forefront of everybody's attention. There are many different superhero duos out there from which you can generate ideal Halloween costume ideas for your twins.

Twins provide lots of fun costume pairings

They may not be Marvel, but the first duo that comes to mind is Batman and Robin. They are the epitome of the superhero duo world, and the costumes can be extremely varied, as there are just so many different eras to choose from. You might also consider a pair from the X-Men or the Avengers.

Dress your twins up in the uniforms of rival sporting teams. Just make sure you aren't asking your twins to change allegiances for the night! In our house, my wife and I each graduated from rival universities so we could likely pull this off without much difficulty.

Think of people from your favorite TV shows, or more importantly, your kids' favorite shows. Most cartoons or children's shows have at least a pair of characters you could use for costume ideas.

The potential for funny Halloween costume ideas with twins is limitless. Get creative and give them interesting and engaging costumes that only twins could make work.

How to Enjoy Christmas with Twins

The Christmas season is a joyful time to spend with your family, including your twins.

Just how ready you need to be will be based on how old your twins are when December 25th rolls around.

If your twins are one year old or younger, then don't worry too much. You can probably keep things simple and they (and you) will still be happy.

As your twins get older, you'll need to adjust your strategies if you hope to keep a smile on your face. This applies not only to gift-giving, but to navigating the rituals and traditions of the season.

Enjoy your Christmas with your twins

Try to give your twins different gifts and not just all two of a kind. This will help them learn to share and they'll even get double mileage out of the same toy.

If your twins are talking, ask them what presents they would like for Christmas. Don't worry, this isn't cheating. If they tell you, you can get it. Doesn't that equal less stress right there? Be sure to ask each twin in isolation. This way you'll get a more honest answer that might not be influenced by or a copycat answer of the sibling.

After purchases have been made, you can employ one of two tactics: let them forget what they told you they wanted until they happily open it on Christmas morning, or get them excited about it by dropping comments to the effect of "Wouldn't it be so much fun if you received such-n-such?"

If one or both of the twins are unhappy during a family dinner, party, or present opening time, don't forget the powerful technique of distraction. Pull out a hidden toy, fun song, favorite candy, piggy back ride, or give your kid(s) the option of having a few minutes of quiet time in their room to read a book or play with a toy. It won't be long before your little one gets back in the groove.

Enjoy your time with your twins. Perhaps you've been working too much and haven't been able to see or play with them as much as you'd like. Enjoy your time off at Christmas to get to know each of your twin's individual personalities and quirks.

Your normal routine will be interrupted during Christmas travels and celebrations. This will put stress on you and your twins. Roll with the punches and be flexible with what you will and won't do.

Twins require a lot of energy and work, even if they are past the newborn stages. They will wear you out. If you've been isolated from them during the week due to work or other commitments, you will get a full blast of twin-induced tiredness over the holiday. Make sure you get some rest to compensate. Naptime or quiet time is always a good idea — even for parents.

Two little people with minds of their own will not always want to go along with your plans. Be patient. Take a deep breath and your Christmas with twins will be great.

Celebrate Your Twins' First Birthday

When you reach your twins' first birthday, you deserve a little celebration. After all, both you and your twins have survived the first year. Congratulations!

You may be tempted to have a big birthday bash with dozens of friends, expensive gifts, decorations, and entertainment.

My advice? Keep it simple.

You've worked hard over the first year to keep your twins alive and cope with the insanity that two babies can bring into your home. Don't add to your stress by having a massive birthday party.

Fortunately, the first birthday is the only chance in your kids' lives when they have no expectations of what a typical birthday should be like. Your twins' first birthday is therefore your only chance to take it easy. So take it easy!

Smile, you survived the first year with twins!

What should you do about birthday presents for your twins? You don't need tons of gifts. Your babies will want to play with the wrapping paper, then the box, and ultimately, the actual gift. This is a new experience for them and they may very well act upset or frustrated if rushed to the next present.

The solution is to have only a few gifts. If you have multiple gifts, spread them out throughout the day to extend the enjoyment. For example, our daughters opened their presents from their older brothers first thing in the morning. When the grandparents came to visit later that day, the twins each opened a present. We had dinner, and then opened some more presents.

Should you buy two of everything? It depends. By the one-year mark, you'll know your twins' personalities and will know if they can share toys or fight over everything. You'll know what kind of space you have in your home to store toys. Plan your presents accordingly.

We made a big deal of each girl having her own cake. After all, each twin is an individual that just happens to be sharing a birthday with her sibling. While I think separate cakes are a bigger deal as the twins get older, the first birthday could probably have been done with just one cake.

There is one thing that you must do on your twins' first birthday: get pictures and video of them eating their birthday cake. Your twins won't remember anything but you need proof that you did something for them on their first birthday.

How many people should you invite over for the birthday party? My answer: as few as possible.

The people you should have at your twins' first birthday party are the people that your kids are most familiar with and the loved ones that want to witness this big milestone (like grandparents).

Ironically, babies typically develop stranger anxiety right around their first birthday, and even grandparents can be treated like strangers. If your twins are beginning to exhibit signs of stranger anxiety, you may want to take that into consideration when planning your guest list.

You've survived the first year of your twins' lives. Now, cherish this day. Take lots of pictures and video. Don't forget to have someone take a picture of you with your babies!

Soak in the sights, sounds, and yes, smells of the birthday because your twins will never have another one like this again.

What is the best way to celebrate twin birthdays?

Beyond the first birthday, you'll want to celebrate each twin birthday and help your children feel special. Your goal should be to celebrate the uniqueness of each of your twins on their birthdays.

Even though it would be easier to have just one joint party, one cake, one birthday song, one shared present, one of everything, it's not the ideal situation for your twins who will already be sharing most things in life. Their birthdays should be a special opportunity where you are able to provide for each of them individually.

Here are a few ideas to help your twins celebrate a birthday so that each of them feels special.

First of all, I would recommend that you have two separate birthday cakes. You should let each twin pick the type of cake they want, how they want it decorated, colors, style, etc. Then when it comes time to blow out the candles, each of them has their own cake with their own candles that they can call their own.

You may also want to consider singing "Happy Birthday" to each child individually so they can feel the joy of receiving the song and then blowing out the candles on their cake.

If two cakes feel like a lot of cake, you can always freeze some after the celebration, or share with your neighbors.

You should definitely get a thoughtful and unique gift for each twin rather than buy two of the same thing and just give one to each of your children.

Consider how their personalities differ or what they like or dislike or what their hobbies are and then purchase a special gift for each of your twins that matches their unique personalities.

When it is your birthday, you should be able to choose what you want to do that day, right? Let each child select an activity that he or she would like to do on that day. Maybe one twin has an activity in the morning and the other in the evening or you can think up another rotation that may work for your situation.

You may be tempted to do a two-for-one birthday party for your twins because they were born on the same day. You should be able to have the same birthday party for them, right?

If your twins are going to have a birthday party with friends or family, encourage those guests to bring cards or gifts for each twin. If your twins have common friends, they may want to have one party with all of their friends together. If you have girl/boy twins, you'll likely find yourself hosting two separate parties, especially by the time they are school age.

If you have a special birthday meal on the birthday let each child select what they'd like for dinner or for lunch. This may mean, just like activities, that maybe a twin can choose the meal for breakfast, and the other twin can chose it for lunch or for dinner, or vice versa. But let each twin be able to select something special that they'd like to have for a meal on their birthday.

One thing to keep in mind: Even though you have twins, and you would think you need double of everything for a birthday party, it's OK to keep your twins' birthday celebrations simple.

This, of course, is mostly for your sanity, but will also help keep things focused on your kids and celebrating them, and not necessarily on all the logistics around the celebration.

I know if you take the extra effort to make your twins' birthday a special one, it will be something that they remember for a long time.

The rest of the year you will have plenty of opportunities to group your twins and activities together, but on their birthday they deserve a special day for them, to show them how much you care and love each of them individually.

A Dad's Perspective on the Twins' First Year

Once you celebrate your twins' first birthday, you can breathe a sigh of relief. You made it. You did it. You survived.

Looking back at my twin daughters' first year, I'm amazed at how quickly the time went.

The first year is an evolution, not just for the twins, but for you as a dad.

When we found out we were having twins, I was in shock. Even after the girls were born, I'd find myself in disbelief that we had two little babies. Now, it is no longer an anomaly, but rather a part of life and I can't imagine life without my little girls.

When we'd go out as a family or travel, people would stop and stare at our twins in the double stroller. I was so used to having my girls with me that I was surprised that they drew so much attention. (Well, they are cute, after all…)

Since we had identical girls, I started out paranoid that I couldn't always tell them apart. As the months went on, I was disappointed with myself as a dad when I couldn't immediately identify which baby girl that was across the room.

However, even from the beginning, each girl had a distinct personality. This continued to blossom and develop to the point where they physically look different to me now because of their personality, actions, and mannerisms.

It was a joyful realization when I could answer the "how do you tell them apart?" question with a simple "I just know."

The logistics of handling two babies at the same time was one of the hardest things I've ever done. Sleep deprivation, rapid-fire diaper changes, feedings, burpings, naps, etc. all took a physical and mental toll on my wife and me.

But guess what? Your twins don't stay babies forever. By the first year mark, the feeling of being overwhelmed has been replaced by more independent little babies, healthy habits, schedules, and the beginnings of communication.

Now you're in a sweet spot of just making sure your twins get their food, sleep, and diapers changed. You figured out how to do all those things long ago, and now they are routine. You can enjoy interacting with your twins and not have to worry as much about how to take care of them.

I'm sure I made mistakes, but if I check those against my primary goals–keep my girls (wife included) alive, healthy, and happy–I think we did fine. I know my girls approved because they'd happily squawk "dada" while scooting over the floor to me when I got home from work.

When I look back at my girls' first year, I have just one big regret. I didn't get more pictures of the two of them and me together. I was usually the photographer and thus rarely found myself in front of the camera.

No matter the regrets or successes of your twins' first year, now is the time to set yourself up for success. Going into the twins' second year, you can correct what you feel is amiss and add in the new traditions and routines you feel are important.

If you weren't around as much as you wanted to be in your babies' first year, make a change now. They won't remember that first year. You will.

As your twins get older, they will remember more that will stick with them for a lifetime. Will they remember you being there? Let's hope so.

CONCLUSION

You'll probably hear incredulous comments from non-twin parents like, "How do you do it?"

Well, as with anything in life, you find a way. That way contains the secret to doing anything with twins.

The secret? One at a time.

Need to change a poopy diaper on both twins? Change one at a time.

Are both babies crying and you're home alone? Soothe one at a time.

Spoon feeding both twins dinner? Take turns: one at a time.

Very rarely will you need to do whatever you are doing simultaneously with both twins. One exception would be if your house is on fire. Grab both twins and get out.

Need to load the twins into the car? One at a time.

Need to teach them how to walk? Walking one at a time will make your life a lot easier.

Time to potty train? One at a time.

Remember, twins may come two at a time but that doesn't mean they need to do everything at the same time.

Just think, they weren't even born at the same exact time. How did they arrive? One at a time.

Things I Didn't Expect with Twins

There have been some aspects of raising twins that are par for the course and pretty similar to our experience in raising our singletons. However, there have been some surprising things about twins, as well.

I have been surprised:

- By how many diapers we'd go through. It seems that they got used up as fast as we could buy them.
- That I'd ever be able to tell my identical twin girls apart at a glance
- That my other kids were able to tell the twin girls apart before I could
- That sleep deprivation was worse than with a singleton baby
- By how many people gawk at our family when we are all out in public
- That the girls do so many things the same and yet are so different
- By just how much we'd need that twin double stroller to control the chaos in public
- By how big and uncomfortable my wife would get during pregnancy
- By how little time or energy I've had to do anything but clean up the house after the kids are all in bed
- By the mountains of laundry that stack up on laundry day
- By the sheer amount of toys two toddlers can unleash in less than five minutes
- That I haven't been able to figure out a way to have both twins help me cook in the kitchen (i.e., make cookies) at the same time
- By how much time it takes to get shoes on, jackets on, diaper bag packed, and everyone loaded into their car seats before we're ready to go somewhere

- At the amount of patience having two sick twins at the same time requires
- By how happy I am to be greeted by two happy faces who run to me for hugs and kisses when I get home from work
- By how truly satisfying being a parent of twins is

Positives of Having Twins

If you focus on the hardness of your new life with twins, it will be hard, without a doubt. However, if you acknowledge that it will be hard, but try to look for the moments of joy that you have, your experience will be profoundly different.

Try to shift your mindset away from focusing on the negative toward focusing on the positive. That way, your days will go a little bit easier.

I love my twin girls and am so grateful they joined our family. Why? Many reasons. Some of which I didn't realize would be the case when this whole crazy journey began.

When our girls were born, I didn't really know what we were getting into. Sure, we'd talked to other parents of twins and read some books. I thought we had learned and prepared.

However, I soon realized that twins aren't just a challenge, they are priority makers. The demands of infant twins (and even through the first year) forced me to realize what is important in life. Hobbies, leisure, sleep, work, etc. all fell down the list of "important" things.

I'm grateful for the insight into priorities having twins has brought me.

When people find out you are having twins, they often ask "Do twins run in your family?" We like to retort, "They do now!" Infant twins have you constantly on the go, caring, feeding, and nurturing them. As they get older, your twins literally run all over the place – and often in different directions!

I'm grateful our twins are different. I love how they are so different to me and yet easily confuse others as to who is who.

I'm grateful that our twins have been an adventure. They keep us on our toes and force us to be flexible and creative in our parenting.

You Can Do This

Raising your twins from newborns through potty training is likely the hardest thing you'll ever do. The first several months with twins is unlike anything else. It is as if you are in a constant war zone, sleep deprived and exhausted without ever getting reinforcements or a break from the battlefront.

Through the difficulties of infant twins to the challenges of actually teaching them and raising them as self-sufficient people, you've got a lot of responsibilities on your shoulders.

You wouldn't have read this book if you didn't care about and love your twins. You want to help them, assist your wife, and survive the challenges you face.

Take each day one at a time and build on the successes of yesterday. See what works, be flexible, and you'll make it.

Welcome to the elite fraternity of fathers of twins. You're awesome.

Additional Resources for Fathers of Twins

As stated in the purpose of this book, other than what you're reading right now, there are very few resources for twin dads. However, here are some additional sources of information that I've found helpful.

Books

These books have made my life as a father—and a father of twins—infinitely easier than it would have been had I not read them:

- *The Sleep Lady's Good Night, Sleep Tight: Gentle Proven Solutions to Help Your Child Sleep Well and Wake Up Happy,* Kim West
- *Healthy Sleep Habits, Happy Twins,* Marc Weissbluth
- *Secrets of the Baby Whisperer: How to Calm, Connect, and Communicate with Your Baby*, Tracy Hogg
- *The New Father: A Dad's Guide to the First Year*, Armin Brott
- *Raising Twins: From Pregnancy to Preschool*, Shelly Vaziri Flais
- *Twins 101,* Khanh-Van Le-Bucklin

Don't feel like you have to read every book, cover to cover. Look at your learning as a "just-in-time learning."

If the doctor tells you about a condition or concern, then go learn about it and dig into the details.

Online Forums

In addition to books, try searching online or posting in an online forum. Sometimes the best answers come from other parents that have been in your exact same shoes.

I've got an exclusive forum for fathers of twins where you can ask questions, get answers, and share what is working in your family. Join the community at: community.dadsguidetotwins.com

Babycenter.com has forums for parents of twins and even subgroups for those with due dates in certain months. You'll find mostly mothers here but even dads can extract some tips on how to keep Mom happy and help with the twins.

Twinstuff.com community offers quick answers to your questions and even has a sub-forum for dads.

Social Media

If you prefer to have your twin info streaming to you via Facebook, check out these groups about twins:

- Multiples and More
- Twiniversity
- Twin Pregnancy And Beyond
- Twin Parenthood

Are you on Twitter? I'm @twindadjoe.

If you enjoy listening to podcasts, Positive Parenting by author and parenting expert Armin Brott offers weekly insights and guidance on parenting: mrdad.com. You can also listen to my Dad's Guide to Twins podcast available at twindadpodcast.com.

Picture Credits

Unless otherwise noted, pictures by the author.

Back cover picture of author and daughters by Kate Fredrickson.

Family picture by Rachel Campos.

Get More Twin Tips Online

Thank you for reading my book! In addition to the resources mentioned throughout this book, you'll find several additional free resources that are accessible online:

- Free weekly newsletter to help you be a better parent of twins
- Specific twin gear recommendations to help you get the best products for your twins and eliminate the stress of shopping
- Dad's Guide to Twins podcast so you can listen to tips and tricks wherever you are
- Exclusive online community for father of twins to learn from each other

To access these resources, visit:

www.dadsguidetotwins.com/more

32800012R00159

Made in the USA
Middletown, DE
18 June 2016